Rawlicious at Home

appetite
by RANDOM HOUSE

Rawlicious at Home

More than 100 Raw, Vegan and Gluten-free Recipes to Make You Feel Great

Chelsea Clark & Angus Crawford

We'd like to dedicate this book to every single person who has ever walked into Rawlicious and tried something from our kitchens. It's a tremendous compliment and in return we vow every day to deliver the best-tasting, healthiest food possible to our customers!

. . . .

Appetite by Random House® is a registered trademark of Random House LLC

Library and Archives of Canada Cataloguing in Publication is available upon request

ISBN: 978-0-449-01618-3
eBook ISBN: 978-0-449-01619-0

Book design: Jennifer Lum
Photography: Rohit Seth
Printed and bound in China

Published in Canada by Appetite by Random House®,
a division of Random House of Canada Limited,
a Penguin Random House Company

www.randomhouse.ca

10 9 8 7 6 5 4 3 2 1

Contents

Drinks and Smoothies   1

Breakfasts   19

Introduction

How often do you find a completely new way to prepare great-tasting food? And how often do you find an easy new way to prepare great-tasting food that's also good for you and good for the planet? Welcome to the world of raw food!

Preparing wholesome, delicious meals from raw foods is easier than you might think. This book will help you discover how fun, creative and energizing a raw-food lifestyle can be! We've included more than 100 raw-food recipes to help you get started. They've all been tested and tasted, and most have been served in our Rawlicious restaurants at one time or another. Some are old favorites with our customers, and some are newer additions to the menus. But they're all intended to inspire you to expand your healthy-eating repertoire in the simplest of ways.

We're big fans of simplicity. At Rawlicious, we want our food to remain consistently flavorful, delicious and satisfying, regardless of who is preparing it. For that reason, we don't have any formally certified chefs in our restaurant kitchens. We hope that simplicity will soak into your kitchen experience, too, and that you'll find our recipes a breeze to make. While a few of the techniques and some of the equipment in this book may be new to you, we're sure you'll find the recipes straightforward and the ingredients easy to find. It is important to note that some of the recipes in this book require soaking nuts and seeds overnight or dehydrating an item for a day or more. As a general rule, always try to be organized and plan ahead when preparing raw meals.

How We Got Started

We've found that most people are motivated to embrace a raw-food—essentially vegan—lifestyle due to concerns about either health or animal rights. Most often, they eventually embrace and promote the diet for both reasons. In 2008, a health crisis in Angus's family prompted a rethink of the family's eating habits, and learning to put together healthful meals became an essential skill. For Chelsea, living with a vegan roommate meant cooking meat was uncomfortable. Six years later, we have become passionate advocates for raw veganism because we've both seen its positive impact on the people we know and love and on the planet we all share.

While we respect everyone's right to choose, we have one simple question: Do you feel good about what you eat? It's the only question you need to ask to figure out if what you're eating is right for you. It's okay for the answer to be "no" once in a while, just as long as it's more often "yes"! To us, feeling good about what we eat means making better choices, having more energy and helping the environment.

About Rawlicious

When we opened the first Rawlicious in 2008, our customers were almost all raw-food enthusiasts. Now we attract a broader clientele, people who are simply looking to eat something more healthful. At Rawlicious everyone can find something delicious to eat. Whether you're a regular and always eat raw, vegan food, or you're a carnivore wanting a change from red meat, when you sit down in one of our restaurants, you're guaranteed a great meal!

Why Raw?

More and more people are soaking nuts, sprouting seeds, and blending fruit at warp speeds. Why all the hype about raw food? And what's the motivating factor behind this lifestyle? We have done extensive reading into the research behind raw food, and what follows is our understanding of the basic science behind it.

First off "raw food" and "living foods" refer to the same thing. Any food that has not been cooked, processed or altered with heat above 118°F would fall into either of these categories. For most people, raw foods do not include any animal products; however, there are some who consume raw dairy, and even meat.

Living food has the power to transform our bodies from the inside out. It cleans out toxins and impurities and can help heal chronic illnesses or injuries. One of the best examples of its potential to heal is chronicled in the film *Simply Raw: Reversing Diabetes in 30 Days*, which documents US physician Dr. Gabriel Cousens's success at controlling diabetes with a raw-food diet and eliminating or greatly reducing his diabetic patients' needs for medication. Also, the world's largest nutrition study, the China Study, conducted in 2005 by Dr. T. Colin Campbell of Cornell University, demonstrated the power of a plant-based, vegan diet to reverse or prevent chronic diseases.

Our cells are living organisms, full of the vital energy needed to perform essential functions. By eating raw, nutrient-rich food, we are providing our bodies with the best possible foundation for carrying out these tasks. Our bodies are beautifully designed for survival, but we deprive our cells of tremendous amounts of potential if we eat food that drains our energy reserves. When we eat food that's been heated to high temperatures or exposed to synthetic chemicals, instead of each cell carrying out its designated function, its first priority is to rid the body of harmful toxins from the very foods we think are providing nutrition. Every day, much of our bodies' energy is devoted to digestion. This energy drain is evident in the sluggish feeling we experience after eating any meal, let alone a big feast like a Thanksgiving dinner. Instead of energizing our bodies with food, we are depleting its reserves.

People following a typical North American diet, known as the Standard American Diet (SAD), consume food that is lacking enzymes, meaning their bodies must rely heavily on their own enzyme stores to make up this deficit. By eating food that's alive and still contains all its natural enzymes, we spare the body from having to tap into its own resources. This not only leaves us feeling energized and inspired instead of sluggish and lethargic, but also frees up energy to tend to other areas of the body that need attention—repairing an injury, for instance.

About Enzymes

Enzymes are proteins that control every single chemical reaction that occurs in our bodies. We each have an estimated 75,000 distinct types of enzymes, including metabolic enzymes (which are responsible for all the chemical reactions in our bodies) and digestive enzymes in our gut. According to alternative medicine expert Dr. Joseph M. Mercola, we are each born with a fixed number of enzymes and cannot replenish our stores. Many of the normal signs of aging are thought to be attributable to diminishing enzyme levels in the body.

Luckily, enzymes are also present in raw foods. The "raw" part is important to note. Enzymes are extremely powerful but their activity decreases in the presence of heat. At temperatures above 118°F, the enzyme is denatured, which means it can no longer function properly. Eating a diet high in raw foods provides all of the enzymes needed for digestion, leaving that precious quantity we are born with for other, more important tasks.

A Practical Guide to Eating Raw and Eating Well

If you took up running, imagine how much fitter you'd be if you ran at least three times a week instead of just once a week. The same goes for eating raw food: the more often you do it, the better you will look and feel. However, we know it's unrealistic to expect anyone to change to a 100 percent raw-food diet. We know first-hand how weird it feels to tote salad dressing in your purse when you leave the house, or to explain nut-loaf patties to someone at work.

Our goal is to have people incorporate raw, living foods into their daily lives. That's it! Not switch to only raw food overnight, not consume only raw food, not give up wine forever! Most of the customers who come to our restaurants are not raw-foodies—they probably aren't even vegetarian—they're just looking for something healthful to eat. If the only goal you doggedly pursue is eating one or two raw meals each day, you'll find yourself craving raw food more and more and cooked food less and less. But it's still okay to make a pasta dinner one night or—gasp!—even pizza. When a pasta or pizza craving hits us, we don't beat up on ourselves, but we do fix a gluten- and dairy-free option and keep it as organic as possible. We also find that at our next meal we're craving a huge green juice!

Just remember our one simple rule: It's all about feeling good about what you eat! Do that more often than not and you'll be on the path to meeting your goals, feeling better and being healthier!

Raw-Food Primer

Here are some tips we've found helpful on our raw-food journey:

Drink filtered water, and lots of it

The human body is almost 70 percent water so we need good, clean water regularly. One of the best things you can do to improve your health is drink a big glass of water first thing in the morning—add a lemon slice for extra detoxification. In our restaurants we use a dual-stage filter to treat tap water because some city water straight from the faucet smells like a swimming pool and can contain a host of things you would never normally drink. Depending on where you live, these could

include traces of pharmaceutical drugs, chlorine, fluoride, pesticides, gasoline . . . The list goes on and does not make for enjoyable reading.

Buy a juicer and use it often

Green juices are one of the healthiest things (after filtered water) that you can drink, but you'll need a juicer to make them. There's nothing more satisfying than freshly pressed juice, and the combinations you can create are endless! See page xix for more information on buying a juicer. Incidentally, we always use fresh lemon juice in our recipes. Bottled juice is pasteurized, which kills any living cells in the juice.

Drink your salads . . . and eat one every day

One of the common myths about those of us who eat raw is that we all live on just carrot sticks and celery sticks. While we demonstrate in this book that there's way more to eat than crudités, vegetables—especially in the form of salads—should be a mainstay of your diet. A green smoothie is a great way to literally drink your salad, and have it taste like a fruit smoothie to boot! Another good habit to get into is eating a big salad at least once a day; nothing is more satisfying. Keeping a salad dressing or two in your fridge makes it even easier to fix a salad every day, and you can make large batches of our dressings that keep fresh for two to three weeks.

Choose organic

Our restaurants use organic ingredients as much as possible and you should too. Recipes taste so much better when made with organic produce, and the environment benefits when toxic chemicals aren't involved in agriculture. No amount of rinsing can undo the damage inflicted on ingredients grown under chemical attack. We're always grateful to have the option of buying organic fruits and vegetables and supporting the farmers who grow their crops in an environmentally friendly way.

Use fresh herbs when possible

Fresh herbs add pizzazz to any recipe. Once you get accustomed to cooking with them, you'll develop your own favorite combos.

Use sea salt but not too much of it

We use very little salt in our recipes and only enough to enhance the taste. When we do use it, we make sure it's pink Himalayan sea salt (see page xxiv).

Use a sweetener you feel good about

We can't deny ourselves the pleasure gourmet desserts give us and, although fruit is the most delicious sweet thing there is, recipes sometimes call for a sweetener. We use agave nectar in our recipes but if you prefer to use dates, maple syrup or a low-calorie sweetener like yacón, go ahead! The most important thing is to feel good about what you eat and have your body agree with you. You will need to play around with the sweetness of a recipe should you decide to switch out the agave. Always start off with a small amount—you can always add more, but it's harder to take it back if it's too much!

Soak your nuts and seeds

Nature is very wise and prevents nuts and seeds from sprouting and growing into their respective plants until it rains. Once water's added, the germination process begins and the nutrient density intensifies. Almost all of the nuts and seeds we use are soaked, and each one has a specific soaking time (see chart). To soak nuts or seeds, put them in a bowl with enough room-temperature filtered water to cover them by about 3 inches, then let them stand, uncovered, at room temperature for the time specified. The longer you soak them, the more water they will take in; however, the 3-inch rule ensures there is always enough water and room for hydration and expansion.

The times given are for minimum soaking time but you can soak for longer if you wish. We generally don't soak anything for longer than 12 hours.

ITEM	TIME REQUIRED
Almonds	12 hours
Buckwheat	30 minutes
Cashews	4 hours
Pecans	6 hours
Pumpkin seeds	6 hours
Sunflower seeds	2 hours
Walnuts	4 hours
Hazelnuts	no need to soak
Hemp seeds	no need to soak
Macadamia nuts	no need to soak
Pine nuts	no need to soak
Sesame seeds	no need to soak

Carry snacks

This doesn't mean you need to pack a lunch box every day, but carrying around some dehydrated chips, cookies, granola or simply an apple is a great way to snack healthfully. Once you leave home, it can be very difficult to find something you feel good about eating, so it's always good to have a snack on hand.

It's okay to break the mold

It's important to give exact measurements when writing recipes but that doesn't mean you shouldn't play around with quantities to mold them to your own taste. Some people are too hung up on following a recipe to the letter and they avoid making something when they don't have one tiny ingredient. Treat our recipes as inspirations instead of step-by-step instructions and you'll soon gain confidence in the kitchen and start creating your own dishes! And remember, often if you are missing an ingredient, chances are the dish may still work out. Raw food offers more flexibility than regular cooking in that way.

Plan ahead

You will notice throughout the book that if a recipe calls for another ingredient that has to be prepared in advance, it will be noted in the "Before You Begin" section before the recipe begins. A key component to raw-food preparation is planning ahead due to the need for soaking and dehydrating. Trust us, once you get used to it and get the hang of it, it becomes second nature! But at first, just ensure that you read the recipe fully a few days before you plan on making it, to avoid disappointment.

Equipment to Get You Started

Adding more living foods to your diet doesn't mean buying a ton of new kitchen equipment. You probably have a lot of the items you need already. This list includes the appliances we have in our restaurant kitchens, but you don't need them all to get started on a raw-food lifestyle.

High-speed blender

A high-speed blender is expensive (around $500), but if you buy only one appliance, this should be it. Any raw recipe that requires a blender won't turn out nearly as creamy and smooth if you use a standard department store blender, and a high-speed blender is essential if you want to make the raw-food equivalent of ice cream. Also, a blender can double as a juicer if you blend ingredients with a small amount of distilled water, ¼ cup or so, then strain the pulp through a nut milk bag.

The two most popular brands of high-speed blender are Blendtec and Vitamix. Both are great, but for home use we recommend a Blendtec. It will take up less room because it is shorter and fits under upper cabinets more easily, and it looks a bit more polished. It's also easier to remove ingredients from the Blendtec jug – the base is wider so you are more able to reach more of the good stuff on the bottom with a spatula. Both brands can be found online, new or used. There's nothing wrong with buying a used blender; it can save you a bundle of money and these machines are built to last for 20 years or more.

Juicer

Juicers range in price from $150 to $800. We mainly use two juicers: the Hurom Slow Juicer, which slowly extracts juice, preserving the enzymes and other good stuff, but clogs easily and is tricky to clean; and the Breville Juice Fountain Elite, which is more efficient and durable. Either one is good for home use. Speedier juicers process ingredients at higher temperatures so you lose some of the enzymes and get less juice. However, they can be easier to clean and are somewhat cheaper.

Food processor

This is one item you might already have. Prices range from $40 to $1,000. We love Cuisinart and use its food processors in all our locations. The only thing to be careful about when selecting a food processor is the capacity of the bowl. If you think you'll be using the food processor a lot, choose one with a bigger bowl. Some brands now come with different sizes of bowls.

Dehydrator

Raw food would seem a lot less freaky if dehydrators were called "low-temperature ovens," which is exactly what they are. Essentially, a dehydrator slowly draws moisture out of the food without cooking it, as the temperature never reaches above 118°F. And when we say slowly, we mean it. The recipes in this book that use a dehydrator require between one to 24 hours dehydrating, so be sure to make note of this before beginning a recipe.

Earlier dehydrator models were round and had stacked trays, which required a lot of opening and rearranging in order to dehydrate evenly. The Excalibur models have the fan in the back to circulate air flow evenly, so we find that there is very little need to rotate trays with this brand. When Chelsea started eating raw and needed to dehydrate an ingredient, she would turn her oven at home to its lowest setting and leave the door cracked open with a thermometer inside to keep an eye on the temperature. This was tough on her roommates as it tied up the oven for days at a time, but at least they got to share in what she was making! Nowadays we have numerous dehydrators at the Rawlicious restaurant, all of them by Excalibur. Dehydrators, which include reusable nonstick sheets, range in price from around $200 to $500, depending on the number of trays they accommodate. All of the recipes in this book are based on nine-tray Excalibur dehydrators.

Ice-cream maker

Sure, it has only one function but for any ice-cream lover who wants to swap their usual dairy version for raw ice cream, an ice-cream maker is essential. Around $100 will buy you a machine that whips any cashew and coconut–based "ice cream" into a delicious frozen treat. But note that you'll need a high-speed blender as well to make a really smooth, creamy "ice cream."

Chef's knife

A good knife can cost between $100 and $200 but with proper care and regular sharpening, it can literally last a lifetime. We use Global stainless steel and Kyocera ceramic knives in our restaurants, and keep them sharp with a Global Water Sharpener.

Vegetable peeler

A peeler is an inexpensive tool but one that we couldn't live without. Use it to peel your zucchini before spiralizing (see below), or your sweet potatoes before making chips. We've found an $8 peeler works just as well as a $20 one, so choose whatever brand you prefer.

Spatula

Some raw-food ingredients can be expensive and you don't want to leave any behind in the equipment used to prepare them. Blender jugs can be particularly tough to scrape clean without a good spatula. We prefer silicone or wooden ones.

Spiralizer

A spiralizer turns vegetables and fruits into beautiful shapes, from chip-like wafers to spaghetti noodles. Priced at roughly $55, this hand-powered device is an easy way to satisfy your pasta craving and show off your raw-food skills to friends and family. Some of our regular customers who don't own spiralizers have occasionally brought their own zucchini to our restaurants and asked us to spiralize them for a dinner party. It's all in a day's work at Rawlicious! In a pinch you can use a good potato peeler to thinly slice broad pieces of zucchini. If you stack these pieces on top of each other you can then thinly slice them into spaghetti-like noodles.

Springform pan

A springform pan has a removable bottom, which makes unmolding things like cheesecakes a whole lot easier. They come in various sizes but we use 10-inch ones.

Nut milk bag

"Milk" can be made from hemp seeds, pumpkin seeds, cashews, almonds or just about any other nut or seed. The most common is made with almonds, which also requires a nut milk bag to separate the pulp from the liquid. A nut milk bag will only set you back about $10. We use ours every day so it's definitely worth buying one.

Mason jars

Mason jars are our preferred method of storage for sauces, milks, etc. They keep things really fresh and make your fridge look like a work of art when all the beautiful colors are lined up on the shelves.

Marinara Sauce (see recipe on page 103)

Stocking Your Raw-Food Pantry and Fridge

When you make the switch to a raw-food lifestyle, the first thing you need to do is toss out all the white, processed items—white pasta, white flour, white sugar, etc.—that you have in your pantry. The second step is to stock your kitchen with a bounty of organic fruits and vegetables and other quality ingredients to cook with. It's time to go shopping!

You'll notice that in a few of our recipes we do use small amounts of some processed ingredients, like balsamic vinegar or vanilla. At times, finding truly raw alternatives is outrageously expensive or simply impossible, so we occasionally turn to ingredients like these to enhance the flavor of a recipe. We use such small amounts of them so we don't consider it too much of a compromise for our approach to eating raw, but if you are following a stricter raw diet then feel free to omit them from the recipes. We also try to create our recipes with items that are easy to find. There's nothing more frustrating than spending hours searching for a barely pronounceable ingredient that costs an arm and a leg and involves a trip across town, only to find you need just a drop or pinch of it. Here's a list of things you should have on hand before you start experimenting with raw recipes—pantry staples for the raw-food lifestyle.

From the Bulk or Grocery Store

Luckily most bulk stores carry raw, unprocessed nuts and seeds. Buy them in small quantities until you know what you'll go through quickly. At home, we decant bulk-store ingredients to small mason jars to ensure freshness and so we have everything on hand. Many of the ingredients on this list can also be found in your local grocery store.

Almonds We use almonds for a variety of things from milk to cheesecake crusts. Always be sure to soak them for at least 12 hours (see page xvi) to make them easier to digest.

Apple cider vinegar This adds a very strong, distinct acidic element to any dish.

Balsamic vinegar This is a rich-tasting, slightly sweet vinegar that we use in salad dressings and marinades.

Buckwheat Despite its name, this is a non-wheat, gluten-free grain that, when sprouted (see page 160), can be used as a cereal or in a crust recipe.

Cacao Cacao is different from the cocoa found in your grocery store's baking aisle. Cocoa powder is processed so you definitely want to avoid it and opt, instead, for cacao. Cacao is raw, unprocessed chocolate. It's available as a powder (cacao powder), butter (cacao butter) or whole beans (cacao nibs).

Cashews This is the most commonly used nut in raw-food preparation. It adds creaminess and a mostly neutral flavor to sauces and desserts.

Coconut meat We use coconut a lot. Shredded coconut, coconut oil and coconut butter are easy to find, but coconut meat is not. You'll need to check out Asian grocery stores for young, green Thai coconuts. These aren't the same as the brown, husky mature coconuts found at your typical grocery store. The young coconuts contain fleshy, white coconut meat and delicious coconut water. This will also let you make coconut milk, the liquid from grated coconut meat—creamy and delicious! Not to be confused with coconut water. You can also take the easy road and purchase frozen, organic, young coconut from a raw specialty store like www.upayanaturals.com.

Currants Currants are like baby raisins and just as sweet. You can use either in the recipes in this book.

Dates The Medjool is the king of dates but you can use any type you like of this great natural sweetener. Soaking dates in hot water for a minute or two softens them up for easier blending.

Dijon mustard This is a key element in a good salad dressing; buy organic, of course.

Dried herbs (oregano, basil, etc.) Organic are best and easier to find than ever before.

Flaxseeds Loaded with fiber and omega-3 fatty acids, flaxseeds are one of the healthiest things you can add to your diet! Try adding 1 tablespoonful of ground flaxseed to your morning smoothie or even 1 tablespoonful of flax seed oil.

Goji berries This well-known superfood is a complete protein source that contains 18 amino acids.

Hemp seeds These nutty-flavored seeds contain all the essential amino acids as well as omega-3s and omega-6s.

Himalayan sea salt This salt from Pakistan contains all the same minerals as sea water. Throw out your standard table salt as it's been processed and bleached beyond recognition, leaving it with no trace elements at all.

Maple syrup Make sure you buy real maple syrup (not maple-flavored corn syrup) and, for the richest taste, choose Grade B maple syrup.

Oat groats Gluten-free oat groats can be found online or in health food stores; use them for making oatmeal or cookies.

Olive oil We use organic, cold pressed, extra virgin olive oil for all recipes in this book.

Pine nuts These are so expensive we weep when we drop any on the floor. Soft and buttery, they're a great topper for salads.

Pumpkin seeds Great as a snack on their own or in cookies or granola, pumpkin seeds are a good source of many good things—vitamin K, zinc and protein to name just three.

Sesame seeds High in minerals like copper and magnesium, sesame seeds add a nice crunch to dishes and make a beautiful garnish.

Sun-dried tomatoes Delicious on pizza or processed in tomato sauce, sun-dried tomatoes add a deep tomato flavor.

Sunflower seeds This cost-effective substitute for more expensive nuts (like pine nuts) has a neutral flavor and a very high concentration of vitamin E.

Tahini This is essentially ground sesame-seed butter. It's great in salad dressings.

Unsweetened shredded coconut This is the main ingredient in our macaroons. It's imperative to buy unsweetened shredded coconut so you don't consume any processed sugars.

Vanilla extract Pure vanilla extract is a subtle yet important flavor component of many desserts and smoothies.

Walnuts Very high in omega-3s, walnuts are good brain food and work well in both sweet and savory recipes.

From the Health Food Store

Agave nectar This is what you should use in any recipe in this book calling for agave. It's a very common sweetener that's sweeter than honey but runnier and with no flavor beyond its sweetness.

Almond butter This is made from almonds that have been processed to a buttery consistency; we use it for thickening smoothies and adding protein to a recipe.

Coconut Aminos Made from coconut sap, this liquid is a great replacement for soy sauce or tamari. It has a smokier flavor than soy sauce and is completely raw. It contains 17 amino acids, the building blocks of protein.

Coconut butter This is coconut meat that's been puréed into a creamy butter. We use it as a thickener in our desserts.

Coconut oil Extracted from coconut meat, coconut oil is an incredibly healthy form of fat. It comprises mostly medium-chain fatty acids, which require less energy to digest than the long-chain fatty acids found in other vegetable oils. It also makes a great moisturizer and face wash!

Kelp noodles The noodles of the sea, these are clear and fairly tasteless but add crunch to salads and pasta dishes and are high in iodine.

Lecithin This naturally occurring fatty substance acts as a thickener, and only a small amount is required to solidify a recipe. We use soy lecithin but, if you are avoiding soy, sunflower lecithin is also available.

Lydia's Seasoning This is a raw, sprouted seasoning blend that we have come to love. It contains a whole host of dehydrated herbs, gluten-free grains and vegetables. It's great in recipes or sprinkled on top of just about anything savory.

Miso Depending on your culture, this ingredient could be completely mainstream or one you've never heard of. Made from fermented rice or barley or—more typically—soybeans, miso is common in Japanese cooking. It's a thick paste that has a salty taste and gives a lot of flavor to sauces and raw-food "cheese," as well as soups. It comes in both light and dark versions; we use light in the restaurants and for the recipes in this book.

Nori Made from seaweed and resembling paper, this makes a tasty snack. We use the unroasted kind for our nori rolls.

Nutritional yeast This may have a completely unappetizing name but it adds cheesy flavor to any recipe! It's an inactive form of yeast so won't behave like the yeast used in baking, and is an organism grown on molasses then processed into flaky yellow particles. Because of this processing, it is technically not considered a raw ingredient but is very common in raw recipes. It's also a very good source of vitamin B12, which might explain why it has such a good reputation in the raw-food world.

Protein powder In the Rawlicious restaurants, we use two types of protein powders. We use a hemp protein powder from Manitoba Harvest and a brown rice protein from SunWarrior. They both pack lots of protein but have very different texture profiles. While the hemp is more nutty in flavor and grainy, the brown rice is more subtle but chalkier in texture. It really boils down to a personal palate difference.

Psyllium This thickener, which is high in soluble fiber, is made from the seed casings of the psyllium plant.

Spirulina A blue-green fresh water algae that is rich in protein and can help regulate cholesterol and blood pressure. We use it as an extra that can be added to juices or smoothies, and also in our Mint Chocolate Chip Ice Cream to give it the green color it requires!

Vanilla powder A great alternative to vanilla extract as it does not discolor the recipe, but gives a rich vanilla flavor to anything it's added to.

The Five-Day Challenge

The simplest way to start to experience the many benefits of eating an all-raw diet is to embark on a raw cleanse and dedicate a few days to eating exclusively raw meals and snacks. If you live near one of our restaurants and want to give the raw-food lifestyle a try, we offer five-day cleanses that run Monday through Friday. Every morning around 8 a.m. participants pick up their food. Each day's allowance includes breakfast, lunch, dinner, a snack and, of course, dessert. Many customers love the plan so much they participate every month and often ask about extending the cleanse for longer.

An easy way to do this at home is to have one of our smoothies for breakfast, snack on fruit and nuts and maybe a green juice or two throughout the day, then enjoy a huge salad, with all kinds of goodies in it, for a late lunch or early dinner. After just a couple of days, you'll likely feel lighter and more energized; you'll lose any bloating you may have had pre-cleanse and you'll see your skin glow and eyes become bright! In our experience, your body will achieve its natural weight over time, cleanse itself of toxins and generally leave you feeling optimistic and good about yourself! Of course, everyone has their own unique chemistry and you need to experiment to find what works best for you, but a predominantly raw diet does it for us.

Here's a sample menu from one of our recent five-day cleanses:

MEAL	DAY 1	DAY 2	DAY 3	DAY 4	DAY 5
BREAKFAST	Granola with fruit and almond milk	Tropical green smoothie and super-food cookie	Fruit salad	Strawberry milk shake and super-food cookie	Fruit crêpes
LUNCH	Soft taco with side salad and carrot bite	Rawitch and an apple	Caesar salad and spring rolls and blonde macaroon	Nachos with side salad and carrot bite	Flatbreads with side salad and blonde macaroon
SNACK	Veggies with Thai dipping sauce	Nori rolls	Kale chips	Banana and walnuts	Veggies with Caesar dipping sauce
DINNER	Caesar wrap	Tropical pizza with side salad	Pad Thai	Mexican pizza with side salad	Taco wrap with side salad
DESSERT	Any flavor of cheesecake	Brownie	Chocolate dipped macroon	Any flavor of cheesecake	Pecan pie

Drinks and Smoothies

Lean Green Juice

Many health practitioners consider green juice to be the best medicine. It is alkalizing and packs more nutrition than you could ever digest in a meal! Any combination of greens can work, but we found these four ingredients to be a simple, tasty blend, with a gorgeous color.

1 cup baby spinach

1 large kale leaf, stalk on

3 stalks celery

½ English or field cucumber, skin on

Yield: 1 serving
Freshness: drink immediately

1. Juice all of the ingredients together in a juicer, adding them in the order listed.

Veggie Juice

Veggie juices are so good for you, but have a reputation for being an acquired taste. Adding carrots to any green juice gives just a hint of sweetness, and for some people that makes the medicine go down a little easier.

2 Tbsp parsley

3 stalks celery

½ English or field cucumber, skin on

2 medium carrots, skin on

Yield: 1 serving
Freshness: drink immediately

1. Juice all of the ingredients together in a juicer, adding them in the order listed.

Vitamin See

A spicy kick of ginger makes this the adult version of orange juice (see photo on page 1). The combination of the straight citrusy sweetness of the oranges with the earthy sweetness of the carrots results in a delicious start to your morning!

½-inch piece ginger, skin on

1 orange

1 apple (we use Royal Gala apples but any type will do), skin on

2 medium carrots, skin on

Yield: 1 serving
Freshness: drink immediately

Juicing the ingredients in the order listed is important to ensure the smaller ingredients are combined properly

1. Juice all of the ingredients together in a juicer, adding them in the order listed to make sure the ginger is well incorporated with the rest of the ingredients.

Ginger Love Juice

This gorgeous deep red juice is rich in both vitamins and minerals—and it's incredibly delicious (see photo on page 1). And beets are more than just a pretty face; they're honest to goodness brain food.

½-inch piece ginger, skin on

1 large beet

½ apple (we use Royal Gala apples but any type will do), skin on

2 medium carrots, skin on

Yield: 1 serving
Freshness: 2 days in the fridge

1. Juice all of the ingredients together in a juicer, adding them in the order listed. A sprinkle of ground cinnamon is a nice touch.

Almond Milk

This is the most basic ingredient you'll need for great smoothies. With a dash of vanilla it can also be great on its own or in your morning cereal.

½ cup whole almonds, soaked

2½ cups filtered water

Yield: 3 cups
Freshness: 2 days in the fridge

1. Blend the almonds with the water in a blender at variable speed until all of the almonds are completely broken down and only small flecks of skin remain.
2. Strain the mixture through a nut milk bag, then transfer it to a mason jar or other airtight container and store in the fridge.

Reserve the almond pulp for use in other recipes (see Superfood Cookies, page 122). It will keep for 2 days in an airtight container in the fridge.

Chocolate Protein Shake

Use some hemp seeds to create a milk substitute, then add a little brown rice protein and, voilà, you have a delicious, protein-packed post-workout smoothie!

¾ cup filtered water

2 Tbsp hemp seeds

2 bananas

2 Tbsp cacao powder

2 Tbsp agave nectar

1 Tbsp brown rice protein powder

Dash pure vanilla extract

⅔ cup ice cubes

Yield: 1 serving
Freshness: drink immediately

1. Blend the water and hemp seeds together in a blender. Add the other ingredients and continue to blend until fully combined.

Be sure to use ripe bananas to help your smoothies taste their best! You can use any protein powder in this recipe, but we like SunWarrior because it is raw and sprouted (see page xxv).

Choco-Minty Smoothie

This one is for all the chocolate and mint lovers out there. Be careful not to over-mint this smoothie, though. The strength of the peppermint extract you use greatly affects the recipe and can mean the difference between enjoying a delicious smoothie and drinking mouthwash! Test it out with just one drop at first and increase to two if you wish.

Before You Begin: Prepare the Almond Milk (page 5).

1¼ cups Almond Milk

1 banana

2 Tbsp cacao powder

2 Tbsp agave nectar

1–2 drops peppermint extract

⅔ cup ice cubes

Yield: 1 serving
Freshness: drink immediately

1. Blend all of the ingredients together in a blender until smooth.

If you want to make this smoothie a little thicker, try adding one-quarter of an avocado or pre-freeze the bananas. To do this, peel a few bananas and lay them flat on an aluminum foil–lined baking sheet. Pop it in the freezer and wait a day or so, then use those bananas in your smoothie for an extra creamy and cold one!

Chocolate Nut Milk

This recipe is so easy and quick that you'll be enjoying it at any time! Be sure to use plenty of ice to make it a super-slushy chocolaty treat.

Before You Begin: Prepare the Almond Milk (page 5).

1½ cups Almond Milk

2 Tbsp agave nectar

1½ Tbsp cacao powder

⅓ cup ice cubes

Yield: 1 serving
Freshness: 2 days in the fridge

1. Blend all of the ingredients together in a blender until everything is combined.

Strawberry Nut Milk

Much more delicious and way better for you than the syrup version we consumed as children, this simple blend of almond milk and strawberries is sure to make you feel young again!

Before You Begin: Prepare the Almond Milk (page 5).

1½ cups Almond Milk

½ cup whole strawberries

2 Tbsp agave nectar

Dash pure vanilla extract

⅓ cup ice cubes

Yield: 1 serving
Freshness: 2 days in the fridge

1. Blend all of the ingredients together in a blender until smooth.

Strawberry Milkshake

This is one of our personal favorites and always surprises the first-time taster. It's an even better version than the dairy-based classic!

Before You Begin: Prepare the Almond Milk (page 5).

1¼ cups Almond Milk

1 cup whole strawberries

¼ avocado

2 Tbsp agave nectar

½ tsp pure vanilla extract

Yield: 1 serving
Freshness: drink immediately

1. Blend all of the ingredients together in a blender until smooth.

Tropical Green

This is definitely our most popular smoothie. The fruit does an excellent job of masking the slight bitterness of the kale. Greens have never tasted so good!

1 cup filtered water

1 kale leaf, stalk on

1 large banana

1 cup baby spinach

½ mango, chopped

1/16 pineapple, chopped (about ¼ cup)

⅔ cup ice cubes

Yield: 1 serving
Freshness: drink immediately

1. Blend all of the ingredients, except the ice, together in a blender until smooth. Add the ice and blend again until smooth.

Creamsicle Smoothie

All that's missing from this is a little wooden stick. This smoothie is so sweet and yummy it should probably be in the dessert section of this book. And it's always a hit with kids.

Before You Begin: Prepare the Almond Milk (page 5).

1¼ cups Almond Milk

1 banana

½ orange

¼ avocado

2 Tbsp agave nectar

2 drops orange extract

Dash pure vanilla extract

⅔ cup ice cubes

Yield: 1 serving
Freshness: 1 day in the fridge

1. Blend all of the ingredients together in a blender until smooth.

Coconut Cooler

This juice is like a natural Gatorade—it's refreshing and full of electrolytes, making it perfect for your post-workout drink or for a summer picnic.

½ English or field cucumber, skin on

⅛ pineapple

½ cup coconut water

2 fresh mint leaves

⅓ cup ice cubes

Yield: 1 serving
Freshness: 1 day in the fridge

1. Juice the cucumber and pineapple in a juicer and pour into a glass. Add the coconut water and mint and stir well. Add the ice cubes last.

Lea's Lemonade

There once was a little red-haired girl who had dreams of owning a lemonade stand . . . and from that dream this perfect concoction of classic lemonade was born! Fresh organic lemon juice makes this really pop with bright tanginess.

Individual size

1¼ cups filtered water

¼ cup fresh lemon juice

2 Tbsp agave nectar

⅓ cup ice cubes

Yield: 1 serving
Freshness: 2 days in the fridge

Party size

20 cups filtered water

4 cups fresh lemon juice

2 cups agave nectar

4 cups ice cubes

Yield: 18–20 servings
Freshness: 2 days in the fridge

1. Stir all of the ingredients together, adding the ice last.

Hot Chocolate

In our opinion, a frothy cup of hot chocolate can and should be enjoyed year-round. This is a great classic version that can be customized to your liking with a few drops of essential extracts.

Before You Begin: Prepare the Almond Milk (page 5).

¾ cup boiling filtered water

½ cup Almond Milk, room temperature

2 Tbsp agave nectar

1½ Tbsp cacao powder

1 Tbsp cacao butter

Variations:

Mint Hot Chocolate: add a drop of peppermint extract

Orange Hot Chocolate: add a drop of orange extract

Chai Hot Chocolate: add a pinch of each of ground cinnamon,
    ground nutmeg and ground cardamom

Yield: 1 serving
Freshness: 1 day in the fridge

1. Blend all of the ingredients together in a blender until the cacao butter has broken down (about 30 seconds).

This recipe works well without the cacao butter, but it's a little less creamy, which is not nearly as much fun! The almond milk should be room temperature, as if it comes straight from the fridge it will leave the hot chocolate luke warm.

Breakfasts

Overnight Oatmeal

Oat groats make this a delicious and filling raw breakfast. Combined with fresh berries and almond milk, it's a porridge lover's delight!

Before You Begin: Soak the oat groats in 2 cups room-temperature filtered water overnight. Drain and discard the soaking water.

½ cup oat groats

1 banana

½ tsp ground cinnamon + extra for garnish

¼ cup boiling water

1 Tbsp Grade B maple syrup

½ cup whole seasonal berries (strawberries, blueberries
   and raspberries, or any mix you like)

Yield: 1 serving
Freshness: serve immediately

1. Blend the soaked oat groats with the banana, cinnamon, water and maple syrup until smooth.
2. Sprinkle with a little more cinnamon and top with berries to serve.

Cranberries, raisins or any other dried fruit
can be substituted for the currants. Granola
is delicious topped with fresh berries.

Granola

When we first started making this for the restaurants, we had a hard time keeping our hands off it long enough to bag it for sale. It's great just dry as a snack, or you can let it soak a little in some almond milk for a delicious cereal experience.

Before You Begin: Prepare the Date Paste (recipe at right). Soak the almonds, walnuts, pumpkin seeds and sunflower seeds (page xvi).

1 cup Date Paste

1 cup whole almonds, soaked

1 cup whole walnuts, soaked

½ cup pumpkin seeds, soaked

½ cup sunflower seeds, soaked

½ apple peeled, cored (we use Royal Gala apples but any type will do)

1½ tsp fresh lemon juice

1½ tsp ground cinnamon

1½ tsp pure vanilla extract

¼ tsp sea salt

½ cup currants

¼ cup unsweetened shredded coconut

Yield: 4 servings
Freshness: 2 weeks in an airtight container at room temperature

1. Line three dehydrator trays with non-stick sheets.
2. Pulse everything, except the currants and coconut, in a food processor until combined but still chunky.
3. Transfer the mixture to a bowl and mix in the currants and coconut.
4. Spread the mixture onto the prepared trays, about 1½ inches thick, and dehydrate for 12 hours.
5. After 12 hours, flip the granola, remove the non-stick sheet and continue dehydrating for 12 hours until it is crunchy. When flipping, it is easiest to place a new mesh tray directly on top of the granola, then turn the two trays over and remove the top tray and mesh.

Date Paste

This is an alternative sweetener and can be kept in a jar in the fridge. It's always good to have on hand for your morning smoothie or to use in other recipes. It can be substituted equally for agave nectar.

Before You Begin: Soak the dates in ½ cup of hot water for 2 hours.

10 whole Medjool dates, pitted
½ cup filtered water, hot

Yield: 1 cup
Freshness: 1 week in the fridge

1. Place the soaked dates and their soak water in a blender and blend until smooth.

Hemp Seed Yogurt

Hemp seeds are very high in protein and have a yummy nutty flavor. Eat this on its own, mixed with berries of your choice or with some Granola (page 23) for a bit of crunch!

2 cups filtered water

1 cup hemp seeds

½ cup fresh lemon juice

10 Medjool dates, pitted

Yield: 4 cups
Freshness: 2 days in the fridge

1. Blend all of the ingredients together in a blender until creamy.

Granola and Hemp Seed Yogurt Parfait

Both of these ingredients are delicious on their own, but layering them in a beautiful parfait glass takes them to a whole new level! This dish makes a delicious snack or tasty addition to a raw brunch. We use a 1 cup/250mL mason jar for this parfait but you could use anything you have handy.

Before You Begin: Prepare the Hemp Seed Yogurt (above) and Granola (page 23).

⅓ cup Hemp Seed Yogurt

⅓ cup Granola

⅓ cup chopped fresh berries (strawberries, blueberries or raspberries) plus a few whole for garnish

Yield: 1 serving
Freshness: 1 day in the fridge

1. Layer the parfait in your chosen container in the following order: berries on the bottom, hemp seed yogurt in the middle and granola on top.
2. Garnish with a few whole fresh berries.

Sweet Crêpes

It's amazing how so few ingredients can make such a delicious crêpe! Stuff the crêpes full of fresh fruit or drizzle some Chocolate Sauce (page 135) over them . . . Nobody could refuse this healthy breakfast.

½ cup whole golden flaxseed

¾ cup filtered water

1 banana

¼ cup unsweetened shredded coconut

¼ tsp ground cinnamon

¼ tsp salt

¼ tsp ground nutmeg

Yield: 5 crêpes
Freshness: 1 week in the fridge

1. Line two dehydrator trays with non-stick sheets.
2. Grind the flax in a blender until powdered. Add all of the other ingredients and blend until smooth.
3. Drop ⅓ cup of the mixture per crêpe onto the prepared trays, and spread it round with a wet spatula. Dehydrate for 2 hours.
4. Flip the crêpes over, remove the non-stick sheet and continue dehydrating for 3–4 hours, watching closely as they can quickly become too dry. If they do dry out too much, lightly wet them with filtered water, using a spray bottle, and allow them to air-dry before serving.

Appetizers and Snacks

Nacho Platter

This is the classic combo of salsa, guacamole and sour cream. Some raw-food places like to pile them all in a gooey mess, but we prefer to serve each component separately so you can customize your own chip. Each bite is a new flavor combination!

Before You Begin: Prepare the Nacho Chips (page 45), Guacamole (page 44), Salsa (page 42) and Sour Cream (page 158).

30 Nacho Chips

3 Tbsp sliced green olives

3 Tbsp thinly sliced green onions

1 banana pepper (optional), thinly sliced

½ cup Guacamole

½ cup Salsa

½ cup Sour Cream

Yield: 4 servings
Freshness: serve immediately

1. Line the nacho chips on a rectangular plate, placing the green olives and banana pepper slices at one end, and sprinkling the green onions on top.
2. Put the guacamole, salsa and sour cream in their own small bowls with a serving spoon in each.
3. Dip and garnish each nacho chip according to taste.

Caramelized Onions

These are great to have on hand as you can add them to just about anything! Pizza, wraps, salads . . . the possibilities are endless!

1 Tbsp Coconut Aminos (or tamari or soy sauce)
1 Tbsp balsamic vinegar
Dash agave nectar
1 red onion, sliced into thin rings

Yield: 1 cup
Freshness: 5 days in the fridge

1. Line a dehydrator tray with a non-stick sheet.
2. Combine the Coconut Aminos, vinegar and agave in a bowl. Add the onions and coat them evenly with the marinade. Let sit for 30 minutes.
3. Spread onto the prepared tray and dehydrate for 1 to 2 hours until the onions are soft.

Caramelized Onion, Cheese and Cherry Tomato Flatbreads

This crowd-pleaser is best served as an appetizer but can also work as an entrée. The combination of the sweet saltiness of the Caramelized Onions with the creaminess of the dill Cashew Cheese makes this a very rich and flavorful dish.

Before You Begin: Prepare the Herb and Onion Flatbread (page 163), Cashew Cheese (page 157) and Caramelized Onions (left).

1 cup Cashew Cheese
2 Tbsp finely chopped fresh dill
8 pieces Herb and Onion Flatbread
1 cup Caramelized Onions
32 cherry tomatoes, sliced in half lengthwise
Ground black pepper
Fresh parsley sprigs

Yield: 4 servings
Freshness: serve immediately

1. Mix the cashew cheese and dill together then spread it evenly on the flatbread pieces.
2. Top evenly with the caramelized onions, and add 8 tomato halves to each.
3. Garnish with freshly ground pepper and a sprig of parsley.

Nori Rolls

This is a simple but fun appetizer you can customize to suit your taste. Un-roasted nori sheets are chock-full of minerals and phytonutrients and are almost 50% protein to boot. Be sure to provide a wheat-free soy sauce for dipping—we use Coconut Aminos in the restaurant. It has a less salty, slightly smoky flavor that complements this appetizer perfectly.

4 nori sheets

1⅓ cups alfalfa sprouts

Thin strips of vegetables (¼-inch thick):

    12 strips avocado

    8 strips carrots, peeled

    8 strips red bell pepper

    8 strips English or field cucumber, skin on

    8 strips green onion, green part only

    8 slices portobello mushroom

Coconut Aminos or wheat-free soy sauce

Yield: 4 servings (24 sushi-size pieces)
Freshness: 1 day in the fridge

1. Lay the nori sheets shiny side down on your countertop, with the short edge closest to you. Wet the sheets slightly with water, using your fingertips.
2. Divide the alfalfa sprouts evenly amongst the nori sheets and lay them along the short edge of each sheet in a rectangular block about 1½-inch thick.
3. Layer the vegetables evenly on top of the sprouts.
4. Roll the nori up tightly, starting with the short edge. Tightly tuck it in around the filling and continue to roll. Wet the open edge with water to seal the roll closed. The two ends will remain open.
5. Cut into six equal pieces. The easiest way to do this is to cut the roll in half, and then cut each half into thirds.
6. Serve with Coconut Aminos or your soy sauce alternative for dipping.

When we make these rolls in the restaurant, we marinate the mushrooms for added flavor. To marinate: place the mushroom slices in an airtight container. Add equal measures of Coconut Aminos (or tamari or another wheat-free soy sauce) and balsamic vinegar. The volume of liquid will depend on how many mushrooms you use; you want them to be half-covered only, so add the liquid gradually. Seal the container and shake immediately. Let the mushrooms sit in the fridge for at least a couple of hours prior to using. They are good for up to 3 days.

Spring Rolls

These spring rolls are super-fresh and healthy tasting. They're full of fresh herbs and served with a sauce so good you'll be licking the bowl.

Before You Begin: Prepare the Pad Thai Sauce (page 38).

The vegetable filling will keep for 4 days in the fridge before rolling. The rice paper wrappers are technically not raw but are still gluten-free and free of preservatives.

½ cup finely sliced purple cabbage

½ cup finely sliced romaine lettuce

1 medium carrot, finely sliced

1 green onion, finely sliced, all but the bottom ½ inch

2 Tbsp finely sliced basil

2 Tbsp finely sliced cilantro

2 mint leaves, finely sliced

12 rice paper wrappers

12 Tbsp Pad Thai Sauce

Yield: 6 servings (12 rolls)
Freshness: serve immediately after rolling

1. Mix all of the vegetables and herbs together in a bowl.
2. Soak the rice paper wrappers in warm water until soft. They are ready when they are see-through.
3. Lay each paper perfectly flat on a cutting board. Place ¼ cup of the vegetable mixture in the middle of the far right side of each, right at the edge.
4. Roll the wrappers up tightly. Take the left half over the right, pack the filling mixture together and continue to roll up and away from you. The side where the mix was sitting will remain open.
5. Serve two spring rolls per person with 2 Tbsp of Pad Thai sauce in a small bowl on the side.

Pad Thai Sauce

This is a fantastic dipping sauce that also serves as the key component in two of our favorite dishes: Spring Rolls (page 36) and our wildly popular Pad Thai (page 100). Note that the tamarind has to soak for 1 hour.

Before You Begin: Soak the tamarind in the water for 1 hour. Mash it with your hands, then strain, reserving the liquid in a bowl and discarding the pulp. Soak the cashews.

Tamarind is also known as Indian date and can be found at your local grocery store in the Asian food section. It comes as a soft, malleable block. It softens during soaking, making it easy to mash to release its flavor in liquid form.

2 oz tamarind (about ¼ package, see note)

¾ cup filtered water

1 cup cashews, soaked

1 tomato, halved

6 Medjool dates

2 Tbsp Coconut Aminos

2 Tbsp olive oil

1 Tbsp sesame oil

1 clove garlic

1 tsp sea salt

¼ tsp ground coriander

⅛ tsp pepper

Pinch cayenne pepper

Yield: 2½ cups
Freshness: 1 week in the fridge

1. Combine the reserved tamarind liquid with all of the other ingredients in a blender and blend until completely smooth and creamy.

Cranberry Sauce

This is quick and easy to whip up any time of the year. It adds something both sweet and tangy to our Stuffing Wrap (page 89), but it's also great spread on Flatbreads (page 163).

1 cup dried, unsweetened cranberries

3 Tbsp filtered water

2 Tbsp agave nectar

2 tsp fresh lemon juice

Yield: 1 cup
Freshness: 1 week in the fridge

1. Blend or process all of the ingredients in a blender or food processor until well combined.

The consistency of this recipe is completely up to you. Some people like their cranberry sauce chunky, others prefer it smooth. Increasing the amount of water in the recipe will make it smoother.

Mango Chutney

This mango chutney is so delicious it could be eaten just plain on its own! Or you can eat it with our Nacho Chips (page 45) for a delicious sweet and savory snack.

1 mango, finely chopped

½ red bell pepper, finely diced

1⁄16 pineapple, finely diced

¼ red onion, finely diced

¼ cup raisins

¼ cup agave nectar

¼ cup apple cider vinegar

1 clove garlic

½-inch piece ginger, peeled

1 Tbsp cilantro leaves

½ tsp garam masala

¼ tsp chili powder

¼ tsp dry mustard

¼ tsp salt

Pinch cayenne pepper

Yield: 2 cups
Freshness: 3 days in the fridge

1. Mix together the mango, red pepper, pineapple and red onion in a bowl.
2. Process all of the other ingredients in a food processor until well combined. Add to the veggies and fruit and stir thoroughly.
3. Let the mixture marinate for at least 1 hour before serving.

Salsa

This one is a bright, colorful recipe that is super-versatile. Eat it with Nacho Chips (page 45) and Guacamole (page 44), load it on our Taco Wrap (page 86) or use it to liven up a simple garden salad. Feel free to play around with the vegetables you include—you can essentially customize the recipe with any ingredient you want!

5 large tomatoes, diced and strained of excess liquid, skin on

1 small red onion, diced

1 green onion, diced, except for bottom ½ inch

1 clove garlic, diced

½ red bell pepper, diced

¼ cup cilantro, chopped

2 Tbsp fresh lemon juice

1 tsp sea salt

½ tsp ground cumin

Pinch cayenne pepper

Yield: 2½ cups
Freshness: 3 days in the fridge

1. Combine all of the ingredients in a large bowl and mix well.

Guacamole

We've taken all of the fuss, and most importantly all of the salt, out of this favorite dish. Three simple ingredients combine to make our incredibly rich and flavorful guacamole. You can't go wrong using it as a dip or slathering it on just about anything (see photo on page 28).

2 avocados, peeled

3 cloves garlic, finely diced or crushed

1½ Tbsp fresh lemon juice

Yield: 1 cup

Freshness: 2 days in the fridge

1. Place the avocados, garlic and lemon juice in a large bowl. Mash with a fork until it is a creamy consistency with some small chunks of avocado remaining.

Avocado Scoop

This is an incredibly quick and fun snack. We love to have it in the middle of a busy, stressful day. Its richness is balanced by the tart of the lemon and some kick from our Rawitch Spice Mix (page 155). While this preparation calls for only half an avocado, ideally you would prepare both halves and give one to someone else to enjoy!

Before You Begin: Prepare the Rawitch Spice Mix (page 155).

½ avocado (pitted with skin on)

Juice of ½ lemon

1 tsp Rawitch Spice Mix

Yield: 1 serving

Freshness: a few hours

1. Score the avocado flesh into cubes, keeping the skin intact (that's your bowl).
2. Squeeze the lemon juice overtop and sprinkle with the Rawitch spice mix.

Nacho Chips

Eat these chips with Guacamole (facing page), Sour Cream (page 158) and Salsa (page 42) (the way we serve them in the restaurant) or add Refried "Beans" (page 154) to satisfy your spice cravings. You can even crunch them up on top of our Tomato Soup (page 59) in the winter!

Before You Begin: Soak the sun-dried tomatoes in the water for 2 to 3 hours.

¾ cup sun-dried tomatoes

2 cups filtered water

1¼ cups golden whole flaxseed

¼ red onion

2 Tbsp cilantro

1 Tbsp apple cider vinegar

1½ tsp sea salt

¼ tsp garlic powder

Pinch ground black pepper

Pinch cayenne pepper

Yield: 4 servings

Freshness: 2 weeks in an airtight container

1. Line two dehydrator trays with non-stick sheets.
2. Drain the sun-dried tomatoes and reserve the soaking water.
3. Finely grind the flax in a blender. Remove and set aside.
4. Blend the tomatoes until smooth, then add the reserved tomato soaking water and the onion, cilantro, vinegar and seasonings, and blend again until smooth.
5. Add the blended mixture to the ground flax and mix together by hand. Only add the ground flax once you are ready to spread the mixture as it becomes very sticky. The longer you let it sit, the more the flax absorbs moisture, making it harder to spread thinly on the dehydrator tray.
6. Spread 1½ cups of this mix onto each prepared tray. Score the mixture into 32 nacho chips per tray and dehydrate for 12 hours.
7. Flip, remove the non-stick sheet and continue to dehydrate for another 6 hours or until crispy. When flipping, it is easiest to place a new mesh tray directly on top of the nacho chips, then turn the two trays over and remove the top tray and mesh.

This recipe requires patience as spreading them onto your dehydrator tray can be a finicky task. You can use either a spatula or your hands to spread the mixture onto the trays. Using a little water on the spreading tool helps prevent sticking. The amount to spread per tray is based on a nine-tray Excalibur dehydrator with a tray size of 15 x 15 inches.

Kale Chips

We have been blown away by how the kale chip business has exploded. They're simply everywhere. And it's no wonder, given how people react when they actually try them. They are the healthiest salty snack you will ever get your hands on. There are many recipes for kale chips, but this cheesy version is our favorite. Make sure they are very crispy before removing them from the dehydrator. There is nothing worse than soggy kale chips!

Before You Begin: Soak the cashews (page xvi).

2 bunches kale, stalks removed

1 cup whole cashews, soaked

½ cup nutritional yeast

¼ cup filtered water

2½ Tbsp fresh lemon juice

1 red bell pepper

1 Tbsp white miso

1 Tbsp agave nectar

¼ tsp sea salt

Yield: 4 servings
Freshness: 2 weeks in an airtight container

1. Line two dehydrator trays with non-stick sheets.
2. Wash the kale thoroughly and set aside.
3. Blend all of the other ingredients together in a blender to make a marinade.
4. Massage the marinade into the kale to evenly coat the leaves.
5. Spread the kale out onto the prepared trays and dehydrate for 12 hours.
6. After 12 hours, flip the kale directly onto your dehydrator's mesh tray, remove the non-stick sheet and continue to dehydrate for another 12 hours. When flipping, it is easiest to place a new mesh tray directly on top of the kale, then turn the two trays over and remove the top tray and mesh.

Sweet Potato Chips

This recipe is a little labor-intensive but definitely worth the effort. It may take a little experimenting to get the perfect thickness, amount of coating and drying time to achieve the ideal snack, but every batch is delicious in its own way.

6 sweet potatoes, peeled and thinly sliced

⅓ cup extra virgin olive oil

1 tsp onion powder

1 tsp garlic powder

1 tsp sea salt

½ tsp ground cumin

¼ tsp cayenne pepper

Yield: 4 cups
Freshness: 1 week in an airtight container

1. Soak the sweet potato slices in a bowl of warm water for 30 minutes to remove some of their starch. Drain and throw away the soak water.
2. Combine the oil and spices in a large bowl and marinate the sweet potato slices in this mixture for 20 minutes.
3. Spread the slices in a single layer directly on the mesh tray and dehydrate for 18 hours until crunchy. No non-stick sheet is required.

Spiced Almonds

There are many spice combinations you can try when making these but the Three C's—curry, cumin and cayenne—are our favorite combo. Be patient and let these dry out to a crunchy, snappy snack. It might be two or three days before they are the perfect crunchiness, so plan to do this when you are running your dehydrator for other recipes.

Before You Begin: Soak the almonds (page xvi).

3 cups whole almonds, soaked

2 Tbsp Coconut Aminos

1 Tbsp agave nectar

1 Tbsp curry powder

1 Tbsp ground cumin

¾ tsp cayenne pepper

Yield: 4 cups
Freshness: 2 weeks in an airtight container

1. Line a dehydrator tray with a non-stick sheet.
2. Combine all of the ingredients in a mixing bowl. Toss to coat the almonds evenly in the agave nectar, Coconut Aminos and spices.
3. Spread onto the prepared tray and dehydrate for at least 2 days. If they crunch when you bite them, they're ready!

Soups

Velvety Vegetable Soup

This delicious vegetable medley of a soup has a creamy, velvety consistency, all thanks to the avocado, hence the name.

Before You Begin: Prepare the Almond Milk (page 5).

3 cups Almond Milk

1 cup filtered water

¼ cup extra virgin olive oil

1 tomato

1 avocado

½ red bell pepper

2 cloves garlic

2 Tbsp cilantro

1 tsp sea salt

1 tsp ground ginger

½ tsp ground turmeric

Few sprigs parsley

Yield: 4 servings
Freshness: 2 days in the fridge

1. Place the almond milk and all of the other ingredients, except the parsley, in a blender and blend until smooth.
2. Warm the soup using a rice cooker set on "warm" or a dehydrator, or on the stove over low heat (we keep our soups under 118°F to preserve the enzymes).
3. Garnish with a sprig of parsley to serve.

Rosemary Red Pepper Soup

This rather eclectic list of ingredients combine into a rich red pepper soup that will surprise your palate! The red peppers lend this soup its deep red color, so it resembles our Creamy Tomato Soup (page 59), but the peppers are much less acidic than tomatoes. The strawberries add a hint of sweetness. Garnish this with a sprig of parsley for some nice contrasting color.

¼ cup sun-dried tomatoes

3 red bell peppers, de-seeded and quartered

2 white onions, quartered

1½ cups filtered water

¼ cup extra virgin olive oil

2 Tbsp agave nectar

8 strawberries

6 cloves garlic

½ Tbsp fresh rosemary

Salt

Freshly ground pepper

Few sprigs parsley

Yield: 4 servings
Freshness: 2 days in the fridge

1. Soak the sun-dried tomatoes for 3 minutes in hot water to soften them. Drain and discard the soaking water.
2. Place the peppers, onions and tomatoes in a blender with the water, oil, agave nectar, strawberries, garlic and rosemary. Blend until smooth and add salt and pepper to taste.
3. Transfer to a rice cooker set on "warm" for 1 hour prior to serving. You can also heat in a large pot set over low heat, stirring often.
4. Garnish with a sprig of parsley to serve.

Confetti Soup

This soup gets its confetti name because of the tiny, colorful vegetable pieces it contains. You'll have to do a fair amount of chopping for this recipe but you will be rewarded with a hearty vegetable soup with a delicious broth.

Broth

6 stalks celery

4 cups filtered water

¼ cup Coconut Aminos

4 cloves garlic

2 tsp Lydia's Seasoning Blend

Freshly ground pepper

Vegetables

1 stalk celery, diced

1 carrot, diced

1 small red bell pepper, diced

2 green onions, diced, except bottom ½ inch

½ small red onion, diced

2 small zucchini, 1 diced and 1 left whole, skin on

1 cup kelp noodles

Few sprigs parsley

Yield: 4 servings
Freshness: 2 days in the fridge

1. Juice the 6 celery stalks.
2. Transfer the celery juice to a blender with the filtered water, Coconut Aminos, garlic, seasoning blend and pepper to taste. Blend until smooth.
3. Pour the liquid into a rice cooker and set it to "warm."
4. Add the diced celery, carrot, pepper, green onions, red onion and zucchini to the rice cooker.
5. Spiralize the remaining zucchini (see page xx) or cut it into long noodle-like pieces, and add to the rice cooker with the kelp noodles.
6. Warm for 1 hour before serving. You can also heat this in a pot on the low setting of your stove, stirring often.
7. Garnish with a sprig of parsely to serve.

Creamy Tomato Soup

This soup goes best with a grilled cheese sandwich and *The Flintstones* . . .
Just kidding—and reminiscing about childhood lunch hours! Truthfully, this is
the closest thing we can get to the out-of-the-can version but it's much,
much healthier and even more delicious. Sprinkle some nutritional yeast on
top for a hint of grilled cheese.

Before You Begin: Soak the cashews (page xvi).

¼ cup sun-dried tomatoes

1½ cups filtered water

6 tomatoes

½ cup whole cashews, soaked

2 cloves garlic

2 Tbsp nutritional yeast

Few sprigs parsley

Yield: 4 servings
Freshness: 2 days in the fridge

1. Soak the sun-dried tomatoes in the water in a large bowl for 30 minutes.
   Do not drain.
2. Transfer the sun-dried tomatoes and their soaking water to a blender. Add
   the fresh tomatoes, cashews and garlic and blend until smooth.
3. Warm the soup using a rice cooker set on "warm" or a dehydrator, or on the
   stove over low heat (we keep our soups under 118°F to preserve the enzymes).
4. Garnish with nutritional yeast and a sprig of parsley to serve.

*You can substitute
half an avocado for
the cashews if you
prefer a nut-free soup.
It still gives it the
necessary thickness.*

Creamy Celery Soup

This recipe went through several iterations until one day we struck gold. Proof that you should never give up tinkering until you get it right. It's also a great use for the celery you haven't juiced that morning!

Before You Begin: Prepare the Rawitch Spice Mix (page 155).

You can substitute half an avocado for the cashews if you prefer a nut-free soup. It still gives it the necessary thickness.

½ tsp Rawitch Spice Mix

3 cups filtered water

½ cup whole cashews, not soaked

12 stalks celery, 10 roughly chopped and 2 finely diced

2 cloves garlic

¾ cup + 1 Tbsp nutritional yeast

½ tsp sea salt

Few sprigs parsley

Yield: 4 servings
Freshness: 2 days in the fridge

1. Place the Rawitch spice mix in a blender with the water, cashews, roughly chopped celery, garlic, ¾ cup of nutritional yeast and the salt and blend until smooth.
2. Transfer to a large bowl and mix in the finely diced celery.
3. Warm the soup using a rice cooker set on "warm" or a dehydrator, or on the stove over low heat (we keep our soups under 118°F to preserve the enzymes).
4. Garnish with the remaining nutritional yeast and a sprig of parsley to serve.

Corn Chowder

A sprinkle of Rawitch Spice Mix on this soup gives a nice salty bite to balance the sweetness of the corn. Everyone loves this soup, and we are sure you will too!

Before You Begin: Prepare the Almond Milk (page 5) and Rawitch Spice Mix (page 155).

2½ cups Almond Milk

4 cups corn kernels

1 cup filtered water

¼ cup extra virgin olive oil

1 avocado

1 clove garlic

1 tsp jalapeño pepper, finely diced

1 tsp sea salt

2 Tbsp nutritional yeast

Rawitch Spice Mix

Yield: 4 servings
Freshness: 1 day in the fridge

1. Place all of the ingredients, except the nutritional yeast and spice mix, in a blender and blend until smooth.
2. Warm the soup using a rice cooker set on "warm" or a dehydrator, or on the stove over low heat (we keep our soups under 118°F to preserve the enzymes).
3. Garnish with nutritional yeast and a sprinkle of spice mix to serve.

Miso Noodle Soup

This is a big hit at the restaurants and is a great way to use kelp noodles! Feel free to adjust the amount of ginger to suit your taste.

Before You Begin: Prepare the Almond Milk (page 5).

3 cups filtered water

2 cups Almond Milk

¼ cup white miso

½ tsp Coconut Aminos

½ tsp agave nectar

1-inch piece ginger, peeled

1 clove garlic

Pinch cayenne pepper

1 cup kelp noodles

½ red bell pepper, finely diced

2 green onions, finely diced, except the bottom ½ inch

Yield: 4 servings
Freshness: 2 days in the fridge

1. Place the water, almond milk, miso, Coconut Aminos, agave, ginger, garlic and cayenne in a blender and blend until smooth. Transfer to a bowl and add the kelp noodles.
2. Warm the soup using a rice cooker set on "warm" or a dehydrator, or on the stove over low heat (we keep our soups under 118°F to preserve the enzymes).
3. Garnish with bell pepper and green onion to serve.

Salads

Tangy Lemon Dressing

This bright, tangy, sweet dressing is perfect for all kinds of salads and works as a drizzle on just about anything! The perfect balance of sweet and acidic makes it one of our favorites.

1 cup extra virgin olive oil

¼ cup agave nectar

¼ cup filtered water

¼ cup fresh lemon juice

2 Tbsp apple cider vinegar

2 tsp organic raw seasoning blend (we use Lydia's Seasoning Blend)

½ tsp salt

½ tsp ground black pepper

Yield: 2 cups
Freshness: 2 weeks in the fridge

1. Place all of the ingredients in a blender and blend until smooth.

Rawlicious House Salad

While some house salads can be bland and boring, ours is anything but! It is brimming with ingredients that not only have a lot of taste and a great crunch but are also super-good for you. The colorful beet and carrot swirls are the visual superstars of this delicious salad.

Before You Begin: Prepare the Tangy Lemon Dressing (at left).

2 large beets, peeled

4 carrots

8 cups spring mix, mixed lettuce leaves

¾ cup Tangy Lemon Dressing

1 cup sprout mix

4 Tbsp pumpkin seeds, not soaked

Yield: 4 servings
Freshness: serve immediately

1. Spiralize the beets (see page xx) or cut them into matchstick-size pieces. Set aside.
2. Peel off and discard the outer layer of the carrots. Continue peeling the carrots into strips until you have 1 cup of carrot peels. Set aside.
3. Toss the spring mix with the dressing then divide between four bowls.
4. Place one-quarter of the beets on one side of the spring mix in each bowl. Place ¼ cup of the carrots on the other side. Place ¼ cup of sprouts in the center.
5. Sprinkle 1 Tbsp of pumpkin seeds on top of each salad.

The most common choice of dressing for our House Salad is Tangy Lemon but feel free to use your favorite dressing—it will taste delicious with any! The sprout mix we use, Salad to Go, comes locally from Sprouts for Life and mixes radish, mustard, arugula and sprouted beans but you can use any sprout mix you have available.

Strawberry Pecan Salad

This beautiful salad is easy to toss together but its many tasty ingredients make it special. The sweetness of the strawberries is complemented by the nutty richness of the pecans and, of course, spinach is packed with tons of vitamins and minerals.

Before You Begin: Prepare the Balsamic Vinaigrette Dressing (page 71).

8 cups baby spinach

¾ cup Balsamic Vinaigrette Dressing

8 strawberries, de-stemmed and thinly sliced

¼ red onion, thinly sliced

1 cup whole pecans, not soaked

4 Tbsp pine nuts

Yield: 4 servings

Freshness: serve immediately

1. Toss the spinach with the balsamic vinaigrette. Divide between four bowls.
2. Top each bowl with one-quarter of the strawberries, red onion, pecans and pine nuts.

All Green Goodness Salad

Some salads are mostly green, but this one is all green, hence the name. It is delicious with any dressing but our favorite is tahini garlic.

Before You Begin: Prepare the Tahini Garlic Dressing (at right).

2 heads romaine lettuce, chopped

1 bunch kale, de-stemmed and chopped

½ cup + 2 Tbsp Tahini Garlic Dressing

½ English or field cucumber, sliced, not peeled

4 green onions, chopped, except bottom ½ inch

¼ cup pumpkin seeds

¼ cup hemp seeds

Yield: 4 servings

Freshness: serve immediately

1. Toss the chopped romaine and kale with the tahini garlic dressing. Divide amongst four bowls.
2. Top each bowl with a quarter of the cucumber slices, green onions and seeds.

Tahini Garlic Dressing

We were looking for a dressing for the restaurant with no sweetness in it. This combination has been one of our personal favorites at home for years, so it was the obvious choice!

1 cup extra virgin olive oil

½ cup red wine vinegar

¼ cup filtered water

¼ cup tahini

2 Tbsp Dijon mustard

3 cloves garlic, minced

Yield: 2 cups

Freshness: 2 weeks in the fridge

1. Place all of the ingredients in a blender and blend until smooth.

Caesar Salad

Caesar Dressing

From its tanginess and creaminess, to its perfect garlic punch, this dressing has taken some time to get right, but we think we've nailed it now.

Before You Begin: Soak the cashews (page xvi).

1¼ cups filtered water
⅔ cup extra virgin olive oil
3 Tbsp fresh lemon juice
1 cup cashews, soaked
7 garlic cloves
1 tsp Dijon mustard
1 tsp salt
½ tsp black pepper
Pinch cayenne pepper

Yield: 3 cups
Freshness: 1 week in an airtight container in the fridge

1. Place all of the ingredients in a blender and blend until very smooth.

If a skeptical customer ever comes in, we always encourage them to try this Caesar salad. It is so fresh and delicious, we've never met anyone who doesn't like it! The onion bread "croutons" are a big hit, especially for those with celiac disease who have missed out on croutons for years, and the Pine Nut Parmesan brings the perfect addition of saltiness.

Before You Begin: Prepare the Caesar Dressing (at left), Onion Bread (page 164) and Pine Nut Parmesan (page 158).

4 heads romaine lettuce, chopped
1 slice Onion Bread, cut into small cubes
2 cups Caesar Dressing
¼ cup Pine Nut Parmesan
Ground black pepper
½ lemon, quartered

Yield: 4 servings
Freshness: serve immediately

1. Toss the romaine lettuce and onion bread cubes with the Caesar dressing.
2. Divide between four bowls and top each serving with 1 Tbsp pine nut parmesan, freshly ground pepper and a squirt of lemon juice prior to serving.

Arugula Salad

This is a quick, simple salad we regularly make at home. The slightly bitter nutty flavor of the arugula combined with the sweet burst of flavor from the cherry tomatoes goes very well with Balsamic Vinaigrette Dressing but any of our dressings will do!

Before You Begin: Prepare the Balsamic Vinaigrette Dressing (below).

8 cups arugula

½ cup Balsamic Vinaigrette Dressing

24 cherry tomatoes, halved

½ small red onion, diced

Ground black pepper

Yield: 4 servings
Freshness: serve immediately

1. Toss the arugula with the dressing.
2. Divide it between four bowls, and sprinkle the cherry tomatoes and onion on top.
3. Season with freshly ground pepper before serving.

. . . .

Balsamic Vinaigrette Dressing

Start with a base of bright balsamic, then add layers of sweet and savory ingredients until you build to a peppery finish . . . Sounds like a good wine description, which is funny, because we find this is almost good enough to drink! It's great on just about any salad we can think of.

1 cup extra virgin olive oil

¾ cup filtered water

¼ cup balsamic vinegar

1 Tbsp Grade B maple syrup

2 cloves garlic

½ tsp Dijon mustard

½ Tbsp salt

¼ Tbsp ground black pepper

¼ Tbsp organic raw seasoning blend (we use Lydia's Seasoning Blend)

Yield: 2 cups
Freshness: 2 weeks in the fridge

1. Place all of the ingredients in a blender and blend until smooth.

Olive, Currant, Nut and Seed Salad

The toppings on this hearty salad combine to create a unique and flavorful taste that is best complemented by our ginger date dressing.

Before You Begin: Prepare the Ginger Date Dressing (below).

8 cups spring mix

½ cup Ginger Date Dressing

¼ cup pine nuts

¼ cup pumpkin seeds

¼ cup hemp seeds

¼ cup currants

20 Kalamata olives, pitted and sliced lengthwise

Yield: 4 servings
Freshness: serve immediately

1. Toss the spring mix in the dressing. Divide amongst four bowls.
2. Top each bowl with ¼ of the nuts, seeds, currants and olives.

. . . .

Ginger Date Dressing

This dressing combines a good punch of ginger with the sweet creaminess of Medjool dates and goes well with salty salad toppings such as Kalamata olives. It also serves as a fantastic dipping sauce for your favorite vegetables like red peppers or carrots.

16 Medjool dates, pitted
¾ cup filtered water
⅓ cup extra virgin olive oil

2 Tbsp fresh lemon juice
1 Tbsp Coconut Aminos
1-inch piece ginger, peeled
½ clove garlic
Pinch ground cumin
Pinch salt

Yield: 1½ cups
Freshness: 1 week
in the fridge

1. Soak the dates in the ¾ cup water for 10 minutes to soften them. Keep the soaking water.

2. Place the dates and their soaking water with the remaining ingredients in a blender and blend until smooth.

Some types of dates may need to soak for longer. Medjool dates are the softest so require only 10 minutes, but honey dates, for example, would require 30 minutes or so. Coconut Aminos can be substituted with tamari or a soy sauce alternative.

Taco Salad

This delicious Southwestern-inspired salad has so much going on it is more of a meal than a salad. In the restaurants we serve it with Tangy Lemon Dressing (page 66) but feel free to use whichever you want!

Before You Begin: Prepare the Refried "Beans" (page 154), Tangy Lemon Dressing (page 66), Nacho Chips (page 45), Salsa (page 42) and Sour Cream (page 158).

4 heads romaine lettuce, chopped

½ cup Tangy Lemon Dressing

½ cup Salsa

½ cup Refried "Beans"

1 avocado, diced

¼ cup Sour Cream

16 Nacho Chips

Yield: 4 servings
Freshness: serve immediately

1. Toss the romaine in the tangy lemon dressing. Divide amongst four bowls.
2. Place the salsa in the middle of the leaves in each bowl and place 1 Tbsp beans in two corners opposite each other. Top with diced avocado and drizzle with sour cream. Finally, stick the nacho chips up right in the very middle, on top of the salsa.

Summertime Broccoli Salad

This is a fantastic summertime side salad. Fresh broccoli never tasted so good! It also goes well with a Rawitch (page 81) for lunch.

1 head broccoli

1 green onion, finely sliced, except bottom ½ inch

1 cup cilantro, finely chopped

1-inch piece ginger, peeled and minced

2 Tbsp fresh lemon juice

1 Tbsp almond butter

1 Tbsp agave nectar

1 Tbsp Coconut Aminos

Pinch cayenne pepper

2 Tbsp white sesame seeds

Yield: 4 side servings
Freshness: 4 days in the fridge

1. Chop the broccoli into bite-sized pieces, removing most of the stem. Transfer to a bowl and add the green onion and cilantro.
2. Place the ginger, lemon juice, almond butter, agave nectar, Coconut Aminos and cayenne in a blender and blend. Pour over the vegetables and mix well to combine. Let the salad marinate for a few hours before serving. Garnish with sesame seeds just prior to eating.

Sandwiches

Rawitch

Sandwiches are relatively difficult to duplicate in raw-food cuisine but we feel satisfied with this yummy recipe. It is deceptively filling and a little sloppy to eat, but man, is it delicious!

Before You Begin: Prepare the Onion Bread (page 164), Guacamole (page 44), Balsamic Vinaigrette Dressing (page 71) and Rawitch Spice Mix (page 155).

1 slice Onion Bread

¼ cup Guacamole

6 slices English or field cucumber, skin on

2 slices tomato

¼ cup alfalfa sprouts

Drizzle Balsamic Vinaigrette Dressing

Dash Rawitch Spice Mix

Yield: 1 serving
Freshness: serve immediately

1. Cut the onion bread slice in half, and then cut each half into two triangles. Spread the guacamole on two of the triangles.
2. Layer the cucumber, tomato and alfalfa sprouts on top of the guacamole, and finish with a drizzle of balsamic vinaigrette and a sprinkle of Rawitch spice mix.
3. Top with the remaining bread to form a sandwich.

If you're taking this for lunch or on the road, pack the balsamic dressing on the side so it won't get soggy.

Don't Be Chicken Salad Sandwich

Coming up with clever names is always a challenge in the raw-food world. Feather Free Chicken Salad was one shot at this recipe name; Creamy Sunflower Seed Mock Chicken Pâté was another, rather clunky one. In the end, Don't Be Chicken is just a playful answer to the dilemma.

Before You Begin: Prepare the Onion Bread (page 164). Soak the sunflower seeds (page xvi).

¼ cup filtered water

¼ cup fresh lemon juice

¼ cup + 2 Tbsp cashews, not soaked

2 cloves garlic

1 tsp salt

2 tsp dried sage

2 tsp dried thyme

2 tsp dried oregano

¼ tsp curry powder

3 cups sunflower seeds, soaked

4 stalks celery, finely chopped

4 green onions, sliced, except bottom ½ inch

4 slices Onion Bread

1 cup alfalfa sprouts

Yield: 4 servings

Freshness: 2 days, unassembled, in the fridge

1. Place the water, lemon juice, cashews, garlic, salt, and herbs and spices in a blender and blend until smooth. Transfer to a mixing bowl.
2. Pulse the sunflower seeds in a food processor until lightly chopped, leaving a little texture. Add to the cashew mixture along with the green onions and celery and mix to combine.
3. Slice the onion bread in half and then cut each half into two triangles. Spread the mixture evenly over half of the triangles of bread (the bottom of your sandwiches). Add ¼ cup alfalfa sprouts on top of the mixture per sandwich and top with the remaining bread slices to form sandwiches.

Caesar Wrap

A collard green makes nature's perfect wrap, and de-stemming it first makes it easier to wrap and eat, as the stalk is quite woody. Paul Morrison, our good friend and the longest-serving employee at Rawlicious, is this wrap's number one fan.

Before You Begin: Prepare the Nut Loaf Patty (page 153), Onion Bread (page 164) and Caesar Dressing (page 70).

1 Nut Loaf Patty

⅓ cup shredded romaine lettuce

¼ slice Onion Bread, diced into small croutons

2 Tbsp diced red bell peppers

Ground black pepper

3 Tbsp Caesar Dressing

1 collard green, de-stemmed

Yield: 1 serving
Freshness: 1 day

1. Crumble the nut loaf patty into a bowl. Add the romaine lettuce, onion bread, peppers and some freshly ground pepper, and then add the Caesar dressing. Toss well.
2. Transfer the mixture to the base of the collard green and roll it up tightly to create a wrap. Use a toothpick to hold the wrap together.

Taco Wrap

This is, without a doubt, our most popular item in the restaurants. It's a great opportunity to enjoy the crunchy goodness of all the fiber and nutrition in a collard leaf in the most delicious way.

Before You Begin: Prepare the Almond Cheese (page 156), Nut Loaf Patty (page 153), Guacamole (page 44) and Salsa (page 42).

2 Tbsp Almond Cheese

1 collard leaf, de-stemmed

1 Nut Loaf Patty

2 Tbsp Guacamole

2 Tbsp Salsa

¼ cup finely shredded romaine lettuce

Yield: 1 wrap
Freshness: 1 day

Finely shredded romaine makes this easier to wrap.

1. Spread the almond cheese two-thirds of the way up the collard leaf. Place the nut loaf patty on top.
2. Spread the guacamole on top of the patty. Top with the salsa then the romaine.
3. Wrap the collard green around the filling and use a toothpick to hold it in place.

This recipe produces a fairly small quantity of stuffing, which can make it difficult to blend in a large blender, so a smaller blender would be a better option.

Stuffing Wrap

We love the flavors of Thanksgiving and created this wrap as a tribute to that holiday. The savory stuffing with the sweet cranberry sauce combine to make the healthiest dinner—it won't put you to sleep like a traditional Thanksgiving dinner does! As someone who would happily eat stuffing as a meal in itself, I can tell you that this tastes even better than the cooked version.

Before You Begin: Prepare the Onion Bread (page 164) and Cranberry Sauce (page 39) and soak the almonds, if using (page xvi).

Stuffing

¼ cup hazelnuts (or almonds if you prefer, soaked)

1 slice Onion Bread, diced small

1 celery stalk, diced

½ cup diced apple, skin on (we use Royal Gala but any type would do)

¼ cup raisins

⅓ cup pine nuts, soaked

¼ cup extra virgin olive oil

1 Tbsp fresh lemon juice

1 Tbsp poultry seasoning

10 sage leaves

Pinch sea salt

Wrap

¼ cup Cranberry Sauce

4 collard leaves, de-stemmed

2 cups Stuffing

1 cup shredded romaine lettuce

Yield: 4 servings
Freshness: 1 day in the fridge (stuffing stays fresh for 3 days on its own)

1. For the stuffing, process the hazelnuts in a food processor until ground. Transfer to a mixing bowl and add the bread, celery and apple.
2. Place the remaining ingredients in a blender and blend until smooth. Add to the bread and nut mixture and combine.
3. For the wrap, spread 1 Tbsp of cranberry sauce along the stalk area of each collard leaf.
4. Top with the stuffing and romaine lettuce.
5. Wrap the collard leaf tightly around the filling and use a toothpick to hold it in place.

Entrées

Thai Burgers

To prove that a vegetarian burger doesn't need to be full of soy or other wheat-based proteins, we have used a mix of mushrooms, nuts and seeds to create a dense and flavorful patty. The restaurant staff wanted to call this one the Angus Burger, but I'm happy to just quietly take the credit for its amazing taste!

Before You Begin: Prepare the Burger Buns (page 161), Pad Thai Sauce (page 38), Marinara Sauce (page 103) and Salsa (page 42). Soak the almonds, walnuts and sunflower seeds (page xvi).

Patties

½ cup almonds, soaked

½ cup walnuts, soaked

½ cup sunflower seeds, soaked

2 cloves garlic

1 portobello mushroom

1 Tbsp Coconut Aminos

1½ Tbsp extra virgin olive oil

2 Tbsp finely chopped red onion

2 Tbsp finely chopped celery

¼ cup chopped parsley

¼ tsp cumin seeds

¼ tsp dried tarragon

Pinch cayenne pepper

Buns and Toppings

4 Burger Buns

¼ cup Marinara Sauce

¼ cup Pad Thai Sauce

½ head romaine lettuce, shredded

¼ cup Salsa

4 tsp diced green onion

4 tsp sesame seeds

Yield: 4 servings
Freshness: 1 day in the fridge (burger patties stay fresh for 3 days on their own)

1. Line a dehydrator tray with a non-stick sheet.
2. For the burger patties, process the nuts, sunflower seeds, garlic, mushroom, Coconut Aminos and olive oil with 2 Tbsp filtered water in a food processor until relatively smooth, leaving some small chunks. Transfer to a mixing bowl.
3. Add the onion, celery, parsley, cumin seeds, tarragon and cayenne pepper to the bowl and mix to combine.
4. Using your hands, form four burger patties, using ½ cup mixture per patty.
5. Place the patties on the prepared tray and dehydrate for 12 hours. Flip the burgers, remove the non-stick sheet and continue dehydrating for another 3 to 4 hours until the burgers are firm but still moist.
6. To assemble, spread each burger bun with marinara sauce, followed by a burger patty, then a little Pad Thai sauce and some shredded romaine lettuce, 1 Tbsp salsa, 1 tsp green onion and 1 tsp sesame seeds.

Savory Crêpes

These yummy crêpes were developed for a Mother's Day special at the restaurant. The crêpes themselves are very simple so it's really the vegetable medley that provides the great flavor profile. Our Tahini Garlic Dressing (page 69) is the perfect sauce and really makes this dish delicious. The crêpes are great served with arugula and cherry tomatoes, drizzled with a little Balsamic Vinaigrette Dressing (page 71).

Before You Begin: Prepare the Tahini Garlic Dressing (page 69).

Crêpes

½ cup whole golden flax

2 large zucchini, peeled

1 Tbsp extra virgin olive oil

½ tsp ground oregano

Filling

2 large zucchini, skin on

30 cherry tomatoes, halved lengthwise

2 portobello mushrooms, thinly sliced

2 red onions, thinly sliced

2 Tbsp Coconut Aminos

1 Tbsp balsamic vinegar

¼ cup fresh basil

1 cup Tahini Garlic Dressing

Yield: 4 servings (8 crêpes)
Freshness: serve immediately (crêpes stay fresh for 4 days in an airtight container on their own)

1. Line two dehydrator trays with non-stick sheets.
2. To make the crêpes, finely grind the flax in a blender.
3. Place the peeled zucchini in a food processor and shred, using the shredding blade. Add the zucchini, olive oil and oregano to the flax and blend until combined.

4. Using ⅓ cup of the mixture per crêpe, form four crêpes on each tray, about 6 inches in diameter. Use your hands or a spatula to spread them and make them perfectly round. The final shape will mean the crêpes are almost touching each other.

5. Dehydrate for 4 to 6 hours, until they are no longer gooey or sticky.

6. Flip the mixture directly onto your dehydrator's mesh tray and remove the non-stick sheet. When flipping, it is easiest to place a new mesh tray directly on top of the mixture, then turn the two trays over and remove the top tray and mesh. Continue dehydrating for 1 hour or so until pliable. They should not be crispy but dry enough that they can be moved without breaking.

7. Line two dehydrator trays with non-stick sheets.

8. To make the filling, slice the remaining 2 large zucchini into ⅛-inch-thick rounds then cut each round into two half-circles. Combine with the cherry tomatoes, mushrooms and onions in a bowl. Toss with the Coconut Aminos and balsamic vinegar to thoroughly coat.

9. Spread the vegetables evenly between the two prepared trays. Dehydrate for 2 hours, until soft.

10. To serve, place ½ cup warm vegetables, then ½ Tbsp basil then 2 Tbsp tahini garlic dressing in a line widthwise a few inches from the bottom of a crêpe and roll into a tube, fold side down so it doesn't unroll. Leave both ends open.

11. To serve, place 2 crêpes side by side on each plate and drizzle again with tahini garlic dressing for decoration.

The crêpes and vegetables should be served warm. Time the dehydrating of the vegetables so that they are ready when you want to eat the crêpes. Or, if you prepare them in advance, give yourself 30 minutes to warm the veggies up in the dehydrator before you eat. Likewise, if you prepare the crêpes in advance, let them sit at room temperature for a few hours prior to eating, or warm them in the dehydrator for 20 minutes.

Soft Corn Tacos

A very popular summer season item on our menu. Something about tacos just appeals to everyone. We think it's the opportunity to eat many delicious things all in one item—Guacamole, Salsa, Refried "Beans." The sprinkle of Rawitch Spice Mix was something we added when we saw staff members eating them this way. It was the icing on the cake!

Before You Begin: Prepare the Refried "Beans" (page 154), Tortillas (page 162), Guacamole (page 44), Salsa (page 42), Sour Cream (page 158) and Rawitch Spice Mix (page 155).

½ cup Refried "Beans"

8 Tortillas

½ cup Guacamole

1 cup shredded romaine lettuce

½ cup Salsa

¼ cup Sour Cream

1 Tbsp Rawitch Spice Mix

Yield: 4 servings
Freshness: serve immediately

1. Divide the beans among the tortillas, spreading them in a line down the center of each.
2. Spread the guacamole evenly over the beans. Top with romaine and salsa.
3. Drizzle with sour cream and sprinkle with Rawitch spice mix before serving.

Teriyaki Stir-fry with Parsnip Rice

This Asian-inspired favorite is something we serve on our winter menu as it is best served warm from the dehydrator. The parsnip rice is a quick and easy way to create a base for many dishes and we like to add some kelp noodles for a little extra crunch and playfulness.

1 cup Coconut Aminos

¼ cup agave nectar

¼ tsp sesame oil

¼ tsp ground ginger

2 medium carrots, peeled and
  thinly sliced into rounds

2 stalks celery, diced

½ red bell pepper, diced

1 large zucchini, sliced into ¼-inch rounds

½ head broccoli, cut into small florets

1 portobello mushroom, thinly sliced

¼ head purple cabbage, thinly sliced

1 large parsnip, peeled

1 cup kelp noodles

4 Tbsp chopped green onions

4 Tbsp chopped cilantro

4 Tbsp sesame seeds

Yield: 4 servings

Freshness: 3 days in the fridge

1. For the marinade, whisk together the Coconut Aminos, agave nectar, sesame oil and ground ginger to combine.
2. Place the carrots, celery, pepper, zucchini, broccoli, mushroom and cabbage into an airtight container and cover with ½ cup of the marinade. Marinate for 1 hour at room temperature, turning frequently to ensure even coverage of the vegetables.
3. Line a dehydrator tray with non-stick sheets.
4. Place the vegetables on the prepared tray and place in the dehydrator for 1 hour, until soft.
5. Place the remaining liquid marinade in an airtight container and warm in the dehydrator until you are ready to serve.
6. For the parsnip rice, remove the core of the parsnip and chop into chunks to fit in the food processor tube.
7. Transfer the parsnip pieces to a food processor fitted with an S blade (the steel blade) and process until the parsnip is in rice-size pieces. As it gets closer to the required size, use the pulse function to avoid over-processing.
8. Divide the parsnip rice between four bowls.
9. Divide the warm vegetables from the dehydrator between the four bowls and top each with ¼ cup kelp noodles, 1 Tbsp green onion, 1 Tbsp chopped cilantro and 1 Tbsp sesame seeds for garnish.
10. Serve with 2 Tbsp warm marinade drizzled overtop.

Pad Thai

Without a doubt, this is one of the most popular dishes we serve at Rawlicious. It's a great entrée to serve to friends trying raw food for the first time as it is rich in flavor and is a hearty, satisfying meal. It's also a joy to look at with its mix of colors and textures (see photo on page 90).

Before You Begin: Prepare the Pad Thai Sauce (page 38). Soak the kelp noodles in filtered water for 1 hour.

8 zucchini, peeled

2 cups kelp noodles

1 romaine lettuce heart, shredded

1 carrot, peeled into strips

½ red bell pepper, thinly sliced

¼ cup cilantro, finely chopped

2 cups Pad Thai Sauce

¼ cup chopped cashews, not soaked

¼ cup chopped green onion

Yield: 4 servings
Freshness: serve immediately

1. Spiralize the zucchini (see page xx) and transfer to a large bowl.
2. Drain the kelp noodles and add them along with the romaine, carrot, bell pepper and cilantro to the zucchini. Toss to combine.
3. Add the Pad Thai sauce and mix thoroughly.
4. Divide between four bowls and serve topped with chopped cashews and onions.

Chili

Chili is normally a meat-heavy dish, but this vegan alternative is equally hearty and nutritious—you won't miss the meat. It can be eaten in the summer either warm or cold, served with the bounty of your vegetable garden, or in the winter, warmed in a rice cooker. Either way, a Flatbread (page 163) or Nacho Chips (page 45) are great on the side.

4 large tomatoes, chopped

4 portobello mushrooms, chopped

2 garlic cloves, minced

1 stalk celery, chopped

1 white onion, chopped

½ red bell pepper, chopped

4–5 sprigs flat-leaf parsley, chopped

1 Tbsp white miso

2 tsp chili powder

1 tsp dried oregano

1 tsp salt

½ tsp dried basil

½ tsp ground cumin

½ tsp ground marjoram

¼ tsp curry powder

¼ tsp ground turmeric

Pinch cayenne pepper

Pinch ground black pepper

1 avocado, diced

1½ cups sprouted bean mix
   (store-bought or grown yourself)

Yield: 4 servings
Freshness: 3 days in the fridge

1. Mix all of the ingredients, except the avocado, sprouted bean mix and 1 tomato, together in a mixing bowl.
2. Transfer about one-third of the mixture to a food processor, add half of the diced avocado and the remaining tomato, then purée.
3. Pour the purée into the mixing bowl with the chopped veg and add the remaining avocado and the sprouted bean mix. Mix well to combine and let sit for a few hours before serving.

Bolognese

Combining our Marinara and Pesto sauces with a crumbled Nut Loaf Patty creates this amazing replica of the classic Italian Bolognese! It is also our go-to menu item for the skeptical boyfriend who gets dragged into our restaurants, as it's the closest thing we have to a hearty meat dish and is incredibly filling. We discovered that several sprigs of finely chopped parsley really help draw out even more fresh flavor in this amazing dish.

Before You Begin: Prepare the Nut Loaf Patties (page 153), Marinara Sauce (below), Pesto (page 112) and Pine Nut Parmesan (page 158).

10 large zucchini, peeled

4 Nut Loaf Patties

2 cups Marinara Sauce

1 cup Pesto

4 Tbsp Pine Nut Parmesan

Ground black pepper

4 sprigs parsley

Yield: 4 servings

Freshness: serve immediately

1. Spiralize the zucchini (see page xx) and transfer to a large bowl.
2. Crumble the nut loaf patties over the zucchini noodles. Add both sauces and mix together well.
3. To serve, top with pine nut parmesan, freshly ground pepper and parsley.

. . . .

Marinara Sauce

This is a great all-purpose marinara sauce. It's easy to make but getting the flavors balanced as we developed the recipe took a very, very long time. It was worth the effort, though. This sauce is extremely versatile and can be used in pizza or pasta, and even as a condiment.

Before You Begin: Soak the sun-dried tomatoes in filtered water for 2–3 hours. Drain and toss the soak water.

4 large tomatoes, skin on

1 cup sun-dried tomatoes

½ red bell pepper

¼ cup red onion

¼ cup fresh basil

1 Tbsp extra virgin olive oil

1 clove garlic

1 tsp dried oregano

¼ tsp sea salt

¼ tsp ground black pepper

¼ tsp dried thyme

Yield: 2 cups

Freshness: 5 days in the fridge

1. Quarter the tomatoes and process them in a food processor with the sun-dried tomatoes.
2. Transfer the processed tomatoes to a mixing bowl.
3. Add all of the other ingredients to the food processor and process until well combined but with some texture left.
4. Transfer this mixture to the mixing bowl with the tomatoes and mix well to combine.

Lasagna

The layers of rich, savory flavors in this dish are incredible. In the restaurants we use mushrooms, but you can make it with any veggies you want. Sometimes we substitute the mushrooms for fresh basil or fresh spinach, or we use a combination of all three! People often think of lasagna as a winter dish, but our version is great year-round.

Before You Begin: Prepare the Cashew Cheese (page 157), Pesto (page 112), Marinara Sauce (page 103) and Pine Nut Parmesan (page 158).

2 large zucchini

⅔ cup Cashew Cheese

⅔ cup Pesto

⅔ cup Marinara Sauce

2 tomatoes, sliced

2 large portobello mushrooms, sliced

4 tsp Pine Nut Parmesan

4 sprigs parsley

Yield: 4 servings
Freshness: 1 day in the fridge

Room-temperature cashew cheese is much easier to spread than cashew cheese straight out of the fridge. This recipe works best if the sauces are added in separate layers, rather than combined into one multi-sauce, as it is aesthetically much more pleasing.

1. Peel the skin off the zucchini and discard. Continue to peel into wide strips to create the noodles for the lasagna. A regular peeler will work for this.
2. Layer the bottom of a square casserole dish (roughly 7 x 7 inches) with one-third of the zucchini noodles. Place them flat across the width of the dish.
3. Cover the zucchini with one-third of the cashew cheese, then pesto, then marinara. Top with a layer of tomato slices and mushroom slices.
4. Add another layer of zucchini noodles, this time laying them along the length of the dish. (Alternating the direction of the zucchini slices ensures full coverage.) Top with another layer of cashew cheese, both sauces, tomatoes and mushrooms. Repeat this to make a total of three layers, laying the zucchini across the width of the dish this time and finishing with a layer of mushrooms.
5. Cut the lasagna into four pieces and top each piece with a tomato slice and a sprinkle of pine nut parmesan. Garnish with fresh parsley to serve.

Turnip Ravioli

Thin slices of turnip make a healthy and delicious stand-in for the classic ravioli pasta. They can be filled with a variety of cheeses, mixed with any spices or herbs you like, but our favorite is this tarragon-infused Cashew Cheese version with Basil Sauce.

Before You Begin: Prepare the Cashew Cheese (page 157), Basil Sauce (at right) and Pine Nut Parmesan (page 158).

 2 large turnips, peeled and halved

½ cup Cashew Cheese

¼ cup fresh tarragon, chopped

½ cup Basil Sauce

2 Tbsp Pine Nut Parmesan

Yield: 4 servings
Freshness: 2 days in the fridge

1. Use a mandoline to slice the inside surface of the turnip into very thin slices to create the ravioli noodles. Try to keep them as large and thin as possible.
2. Place the slices in a dehydrator directly on the mesh tray for 10 minutes, monitoring them closely. You want them soft and pliable, not crispy. Remove them after 10 minutes.
3. Mix the cashew cheese with the tarragon in a small bowl.
4. Drop ½ tsp cashew cheese mixture in the middle of each piece of turnip and fold the "noodle" over. Use your hands to seal the edge of each ravioli, wetting your fingers with a little water to help them stick.
5. Warm them in the dehydrator for 5 minutes prior to serving. Once warmed, drizzle with basil sauce and top with pine nut parmesan to serve.

Basil Sauce

We love fresh basil and wanted to create a fresh green sauce to drizzle on our Beet Ravioli (page 108). This delicious and versatile creation is what we came up with. Put it in a squeeze bottle and drizzle, dollop or swirl on any dish to give it some plating pizzazz!

Before You Begin:
Soak the pumpkin seeds (page xvi).

¼ cup extra virgin olive oil

2 Tbsp filtered water

2 Tbsp pumpkin seeds, soaked

½ cup fresh basil

1 tsp fresh lemon juice

½ clove garlic

¼ tsp ground black pepper

Pinch sea salt

Yield: ½ cup
Freshness: 5 days in the fridge

1. Blend all ingredients in a blender until smooth.

Beet Ravioli

The beautiful deep ruby red of the beets in this dish is accentuated by the creamy white of the Cashew Cheese and topped off with the green of the Basil Sauce. These raviolis make a lovely lunchtime meal when paired with Arugula Salad (page 71). We've also served them in the restaurants many times on Valentine's Day.

Before You Begin: Prepare the Cashew Cheese (page 157) and Basil Sauce (page 107).

6 large beets, peeled

4 Tbsp extra virgin olive oil

2 Tbsp fresh lemon juice

⅔ cup Cashew Cheese

3 sprigs dill, chopped

½ cup Basil Sauce

Yield: 4 servings

Freshness: serve immediately

1. Use a mandoline to thinly slice the beets. You will have some extra slices that are irregular or not complete. Select the best ones and match up in pairs for the top and bottom of each ravioli.
2. Combine the olive oil and lemon juice in a bowl, and add the beet slices. Marinate the beets for 30 minutes to soften.
3. Mix the cashew cheese with the dill.
4. Remove the beet slices from the marinade and lie flat on a cutting board. Drop 1 tsp cashew cheese in the center of half the slices.
5. Lay the remaining beet slices on top of them. Use your hands to press down and seal the edges of each ravioli, wetting your fingers with a little water to help them stick.
6. Serve with a drizzle of basil sauce overtop.

Zuchetti Rosé

For all of our zucchini dishes we use spiralized noodles of zucchini—it's the perfect replacement for al dente spaghetti. In fact, we've heard heated arguments outside of the restaurant with customers insisting to their friends that they just ate "real pasta"! This rich and creamy Alfredo-based version goes extremely well with some salty strips of sun-dried tomatoes and Kalamata olives.

Before You Begin: Prepare the Marinara Sauce (page 103), Alfredo Sauce (below) and Pine Nut Parmesan (page 158).

10 large zucchini, peeled

1⅓ cups Marinara Sauce

⅔ cup Alfredo Sauce

20 Kalamata olives, pitted and sliced

¼ cup sun-dried tomatoes, sliced

4 Tbsp Pine Nut Parmesan

4 sprigs parsley

Yield: 4 servings
Freshness: 1 hour

1. Spiralize the zucchini (see page xx) and transfer to a large bowl.
2. Add both sauces and toss well to coat the zucchini.
3. Divide the zucchini between four plates and top with olives and sun-dried tomatoes.
4. To serve, sprinkle with pine nut parmesan and garnish with parsley.

....

Alfredo Sauce

This rich creamy sauce goes well with zucchini noodles on their own or blended with some Marinara Sauce (page 103) for a sweet rosé sauce as in Zuchetti Rosé (above).

Before You Begin: Soak the cashews (page xvi).

¾ cup cashews, soaked

¼ cup pine nuts, not soaked

½ cup filtered water

¼ cup extra virgin olive oil

2 Tbsp fresh lemon juice

2 garlic cloves

1½ tsp nutritional yeast

¼ tsp sea salt

¼ tsp pepper

Pinch ground nutmeg

Yield: 1 cup
Freshness: 3 days in the fridge

1. Place all the ingredients in a blender and blend until completely smooth.

This recipe produces a fairly small volume, so it can be difficult to blend in a large blender. A smaller blender will make life easier.

Zuchetti Pesto

This dish is a favorite of Jessica Valiant, our Barrie restaurant owner! It is so bright and colorful—it simply radiates health and nutrition. We think pesto is good on anything, but these crunchy, fresh zucchini noodles are the perfect choice.

Before You Begin: Prepare the Pesto (below) and Pine Nut Parmesan (page 158).

10 large zucchini

2 cups Pesto

16 cherry tomatoes, halved

½ yellow bell pepper, thinly sliced

4 Tbsp Pine Nut Parmesan

4 sprigs parsley

Yield: 4 servings
Freshness: 1 hour

1. Spiralize the zucchini (see page xx) and transfer to a large bowl.
2. Add the pesto and toss well to coat the zucchini.
3. Divide between four plates and top each one with cherry tomatoes, a sprinkle of pine nut parmesan and a sprig of parsley before serving.

. . . .

Pesto

The basil and spinach combine well with the richness of the nutty-flavored oil-based elements to make this an all-purpose sauce that goes well with anything. Use it as a dip, mixed with zucchini noodles in our Zuchetti Pesto for a delicious pasta dish (above), or on a Tropical Pizza (page 117).

Before You Begin: Soak the sunflower seeds (page xvi).

1½ cups fresh basil, tightly packed

1 cup baby spinach, tightly packed

½ cup extra virgin olive oil

⅓ cup fresh lemon juice

1½ cloves garlic

¼ tsp salt

¼ tsp ground black pepper

¾ cup sunflower seeds, soaked

Yield: 2 cups
Freshness: 3 days in the fridge

1. Place everything, except the sunflower seeds, in a food processor and process until smooth.
2. Add the sunflower seeds to the processor and pulse to combine, leaving some texture.

Ensure that the basil is completely free of dirt. There is nothing worse than gritty pesto!

Sprouted Buckwheat Pizza

Topped with Cashew Cheese and basic Marinara Sauce or Pesto, our pizzas can accommodate any topping combination you can dream up. One of our favorite combinations is bell peppers, red onion and marinated zucchini. Served warm from the dehydrator, this makes a great lunch served with a small spring mix side salad.

Before You Begin: Prepare the Cashew Cheese (page 157), Pizza Crust (page 160), Marinara Sauce (page 103) or Pesto (page 112) and Pine Nut Parmesan (page 158).

Pizza

1 cup Cashew Cheese

1 Pizza Crust

1 cup Marinara Sauce (or Pesto)

4 Tbsp Pine Nut Parmesan

Possible Toppings:

bell peppers

mushrooms

olives

onion

tomatoes

zucchini

Yield: 4 servings
Freshness: 2 days

Cashew cheese is easiest to spread at room temperature.

If you want to add a green leafy vegetable, like spinach, or an herb, like basil, it is best to do so right before you eat the pizza, and definitely after it has been in the dehydrator. Dehydrating leafy greens leads to very crunchy, shriveled, twig-like items that don't work well on pizza!

1. Use a spatula to spread the cashew cheese across the pizza base, right to the edges.
2. Spread the marinara sauce or pesto on top of the cheese. Top with your chosen veggie toppings.
3. Dehydrate directly on the mesh tray for 30 minutes to 2 hours depending on how soft you would like the toppings to be.
4. Sprinkle with pine nut parmesan before serving.

Mexican Pizza

We like to play with different combinations for our favorite dishes. Looking for a unique pizza one day, we tripped upon what we now call Mexican Pizza. It's delish!

Before You Begin: Prepare the Cashew Cheese (page 157), Pizza Crust (page 160), Refried "Beans" (page 154), Salsa (page 42), Sour Cream (page 158) and Guacamole (page 44).

1 cup Cashew Cheese

1 Pizza Crust

1 cup Refried "Beans"

1 cup Salsa

20 Kalamata olives

¼ cup Guacamole

¼ cup Sour Cream

Yield: 4 servings
Freshness: 2 days

1. Use a spatula to spread the cashew cheese across the pizza base, right to the edges.
2. Spread the refried beans on top of the cheese. Top with the salsa and olives.
3. Dehydrate for 20 to 30 minutes depending on how soft you would like the toppings to be.
4. Dollop teaspoon-sized drops of guacamole randomly overtop and drizzle with sour cream before serving.

Cashew cheese is easiest to spread at room temperature.

Tropical Pizza

At first glance you might dismiss this pizza combo, but trust us, it's one of the most amazing flavor creations we've ever come up with. It's hard to describe . . . but let's just say "simply delicious" is an understatement.

Before You Begin: Prepare the Cashew Cheese (page 157), Pizza Crust (page 160), Pesto (page 112) and Pine Nut Parmesan (page 158).

1 cup Cashew Cheese

1 Pizza Crust

1 cup Pesto

¼ pineapple, cubed, maximum 1 inch thick

2 mangos, cubed, maximum 1 inch thick

1 red onion, sliced, maximum ¼ inch thick

½ cup cilantro, roughly chopped

4 Tbsp Pine Nut Parmesan

Yield: 4 servings
Freshness: 2 days

1. Use a spatula to spread the cashew cheese across the pizza base right to the edges.
2. Spread the pesto over the cheese. Top with the pineapple, mango and red onion.
3. Dehydrate for 30 minutes to 2 hours, depending on how soft you want the toppings to be.
4. Sprinkle with pine nut parmesan and top with chopped cilantro before serving.

Cashew cheese is easiest to spread at room temperature.

Desserts and Treats

Vanilla Hemp Bars

We originally made this as a breakfast item for one of our cleanses in the restaurant, but customers kept asking if they could purchase, so we knew we had to add them to our menu permanently. They are a great source of protein so they make a delicious post-workout snack.

2 cups cashews, not soaked

32 Medjool dates (about 1 cup), soaked for 1–2 minutes in hot water

¼ cup coconut oil

1 Tbsp pure vanilla extract

1 cup hemp seeds

Yield: 12 four-inch bars
Freshness: 2 weeks in the fridge

1. Line a dehydrator tray with a non-stick sheet.
2. Place the cashews in a food processor and process until ground. Add all of the other ingredients, except the hemp seeds, and process until well combined.
3. Spread onto the prepared tray. It should be about ½ inch thick. Press the hemp seeds into the top of the mixture and use a knife to score it into bars 4 inches long.
4. Dehydrate for 2 hours. Flip the bars, remove the non-stick sheet and dehydrate for another 4 hours.
5. Let the bars cool before you break them apart.

Superfood Cookies

We call these our superfood cookies because they are packed with all kinds of nutritional superfoods and they taste amazing. They are more of an energy snack than a dessert, so have one late in the afternoon with a cup of tea to tide you over until dinner.

Before You Begin: Make the Almond Milk (page 5) and reserve the pulp for this recipe.

2 Tbsp filtered water

1 cup almond pulp

½ cup currants

½ cup sesame seeds, not soaked

½ cup unsweetened shredded coconut

½ cup cacao nibs

½ cup pumpkin seeds, not soaked

¼ cup goji berries

¼ cup hemp seeds

1 cup walnuts, not soaked

3 bananas

⅔ cup agave nectar

1 tsp pure vanilla extract

1 tsp ground cinnamon

Yield: 15 cookies

Freshness: 1 week in an airtight container

1. Line a dehydrator tray with a non-stick sheet.
2. In a large bowl, combine everything except the walnuts, bananas, agave, vanilla and cinnamon and mix well to incorporate evenly.
3. Place the walnuts in a food processor and process until ground. Transfer to the bowl and mix evenly.
4. Process the bananas, agave, vanilla and cinnamon until smooth. Add to the bowl and mix well to combine.
5. Drop ¼ cup of dough per cookie onto the prepared tray and use your fingers to press them into a flat cookie shape about 3 inches in diameter. They won't expand, so they can touch each other on the tray.
6. Dehydrate for 8 hours.
7. Flip, remove the non-stick sheet and continue dehydrating until the cookies are dry enough to be moved without breaking (about 4 hours).

As with any recipe using bananas, this tastes better if you use ripe ones.

Coconut Cinnamon Snowballs

These are very easy to make and go well with an afternoon cup of tea. They are perfect for bringing to a friend's house as an after-dinner treat as well! We have these on our menu only in the winter, and once spring hits we have some very upset customers!

1 cup almonds, not soaked

⅓ cup agave nectar

2½ Tbsp ground cinnamon

1½ tsp coconut oil

2 Tbsp + ¼ cup unsweetened shredded coconut

Pinch sea salt

Yield: 10 snowballs
Freshness: 1 week in the fridge

1. Place the almonds in a food processor and process until they are powdered. Add the agave nectar, cinnamon, coconut oil, 2 Tbsp coconut and a pinch of sea salt, and combine just until the mixture forms a ball.
2. Chill in the fridge for 10 minutes to harden.
3. Using your hands, form the mixture into 10 balls.
4. Put the remaining ¼ cup coconut in a shallow bowl and roll the balls in it to coat.

Carrot Cake Bites

These small treats taste like a raw version of a Timbit (that's for the Canadians; donut hole for the Americans)! In contrast to the famous comparisons, they aren't as sweet but contain a delightful blend of spices and flavors. A hard outer shell protects a soft doughy center, and the occasional bite of currant adds extra sweetness!

1 medium carrot

¼ cup almonds, not soaked

¼ cup walnuts, not soaked

½ cup unsweetened shredded coconut + ¼ cup for coating

2 Tbsp currants

2 Tbsp Grade B maple syrup

1½ tsp coconut oil

1½ tsp ground cinnamon

¼ tsp ground nutmeg

¼ tsp ground ginger

Yield: 10 bites
Freshness: 1 week in an airtight container

1. Finely grate the carrot then place it in a bowl.
2. Place the almonds and walnuts in a food processor and process until ground.
3. Add the ½ cup shredded coconut, currants, maple syrup, coconut oil, cinnamon, nutmeg and ginger to the food processor and process to combine.
4. Form the mixture into 10 balls and roll them in the ¼ cup shredded coconut.
5. Place the balls directly on a mesh tray and dehydrate for 4 hours until a hard outer layer forms.

Blonde Macaroons

These are incredibly easy to make and are amazing when dipped in Chocolate (page 129). Eating them straight out of the dehydrator is the raw version of eating cookies straight out of the oven . . . Betcha can't eat just one!

¾ cup cashews, not soaked

1½ cups unsweetened shredded coconut

½ cup Grade B maple syrup

2½ Tbsp coconut butter

1½ tsp pure vanilla extract

¼ tsp sea salt

Yield: 12 macaroons

Freshness: 4–5 days in an airtight container

1. Process cashews in a food processor until ground.
2. Transfer the processed cashews to a mixing bowl, add the shredded coconut and mix to combine.
3. Add the remaining ingredients to the food processor and process until smooth.
4. Add these to the cashew-coconut mixture and mix well to combine.
5. Using an ice-cream scoop or your hands, form the mixture into 10 balls and place them directly on a mesh dehydrator tray.
6. Dehydrate for 3 to 4 hours until a hard outer layer forms.

If you dip the ice-cream scoop or your hands in some water when forming the macaroons, you will prevent the mix from sticking to you or the scoop.

Chocolate Macaroons

While our Blonde Macaroons are the most popular sweet treat at our restaurants, these Chocolate Macaroons also have a loyal following. We don't make them often, but when we do, they sell out quickly! They're not as sweet as the blonde version (page 127) and the chocolate taste is subtle, but they are delicious and addictive nonetheless.

Before You Begin: Prepare the Date Paste (page 23).

½ cup cashews, not soaked

2 cups unsweetened shredded coconut

½ cup Date Paste

¼ cup cacao powder

1 Tbsp agave nectar

¼ tsp pure vanilla extract

Pinch sea salt

Yield: 12 macaroons
Freshness: 4–5 days in an airtight container

If you dip the ice-cream scoop or your hands in some water when forming the macaroons, you will prevent the mix from sticking to you or the scoop.

1. Process the cashews in a food processor until ground.
2. Add 1 cup of the shredded coconut with the date paste, cacao powder, agave nectar, vanilla and a pinch of sea salt to the food processor and process until just combined.
3. Transfer to a mixing bowl and add the remaining 1 cup shredded coconut. Mix well.
4. Using an ice-cream scoop or your hands, form the mixture into 12 balls and place them directly on a mesh dehydrator tray.
5. Dehydrate for 2 to 3 hours until they have a hard outer layer.

Chocolate

The velvety texture of this chocolate is to die for. This is the perfect dipping chocolate for Macaroons (pages 127 and 128) or even chocolate-dipped strawberries! Or pour it into molds to make chocolate treats. Nobody will know that it's "raw" chocolate.

¼ cup melted coconut oil

¼ cup cacao powder

¼ cup agave nectar

Yield: ½ cup

Freshness: 2 weeks in an airtight container at room temperature

1. Whisk together all three ingredients in a large bowl until completely smooth with no clumps of cacao powder.

A fast way to melt coconut oil is to place it in the dehydrator for 2 to 3 minutes. If you want to make chocolate-dipped macaroons, put the macaroons in the fridge for 5 minutes or so until they are slightly chilled. Cold macaroons help the chocolate harden quickly so no puddle of chocolate forms around the base.

Chocolate Crème Cookies

Two chocolate wafers held together with a yummy chocolate crème that has just a hint of cinnamon—a cookie lover's dream. We made the cookies on their own at first but they lacked the sweetness you'd expect of a cookie, so we sandwiched icing in between two of them and Chocolate Crème Cookies were born! You'll have a hard time not eating the whole batch yourself!

Before You Begin: Soak the pecans (page xvi).

Cookies

½ cup almonds, not soaked

¼ cup cacao powder

3 Tbsp Grade B maple syrup

2 Tbsp coconut butter

Filling

¼ cup pecans, soaked

2 Tbsp Grade B maple syrup

2 Tbsp cacao powder

2 tsp coconut butter

Pinch ground cinnamon

Yield: 10 cookies
Freshness: 1 week in the fridge

1. Line a dehydrator tray with a non-stick sheet.
2. For the cookies, place the almonds in a food processor and process until powdered.
3. Add the cacao powder, maple syrup and coconut butter to the food processor and process until just combined.
4. Place the dough on the prepared tray.
5. Cover with parchment paper, roll out to ¼ inch thick and use a round 1- or 1½-inch cookie cutter to cut out the dough. Repeat until you have used up the dough. You should have 20 circles of dough.
6. Dehydrate for 4 hours.
7. Flip the tray, remove the non-stick sheet and continue dehydrating for another 2 to 4 hours. They should be dry but still pliable.
8. For the filling, place the filling ingredients in a food processor and process until just combined.
9. Use the filling to sandwich together two cookies at a time.

You can also spread the dough out on a non-stick sheet–lined dehydrator tray and score it into squares. This saves a ton of time but they don't look quite as cute! And you have to be sure to make the squares uniform so that you can sandwich them together.

Brownies with Vanilla Icing

It all starts with chocolate— raw chocolate, that is. Raw chocolate is unadulterated cacao beans without any additives. Dates and walnuts supply both the sweet and the rich components and, in our opinion, no brownie is complete without a scrumptious icing. Rich, sweet, chocolaty deliciousness.

Brownies

2½ cups whole walnuts, not soaked

50 Medjool dates (about 1½ cups), soaked for 1–2 minutes
in hot water then pitted

6 Tbsp cacao powder

1 tsp pure vanilla extract

Vanilla Icing

½ cup agave nectar

½ cup coconut butter

1 tsp pure vanilla extract

Yield: 8 servings
Freshness: 2 weeks

1. Place 2 cups of the walnuts in a food processor and process until ground. Add the dates, cacao powder and vanilla and process until a ball forms.
2. Transfer to a small bowl. Hand-chop the remaining ½ cup walnuts and fold them into the brownie dough.
3. Press the brownie mix into an 8- x 8-inch cake pan.
4. Make sure the food processor is completely clean and dry and then process the agave nectar, coconut butter and vanilla to make the icing.
5. Top the brownie with the icing then chill in the fridge for an hour or so to allow the icing to set.

Be careful not to overprocess at any stage. Stop processing the walnuts as soon as they have a powder consistency—too long will result in walnut butter.

Chocolate Banana Cheesecake

Imagine a chocolate-dipped banana. This is the cheesecake version. Creamy, sweet, and chocolaty . . . Who wouldn't love this? Obviously it doesn't contain any real cheese in it, but the cashews and coconut butter combine to make this a raw version of the classic cheesecake. This dessert is one of our most popular dishes at the restaurant. We often receive calls asking if it's available.

Before You Begin: Prepare the Almond Milk (page 5) and Chocolate Sauce (facing page). Soak the almonds and cashews (page xvi).

Lecithin is a naturally occurring fatty substance that acts as a thickener, and only a small amount is required to solidify a recipe. We use soy lecithin but, if you are avoiding soy, sunflower lecithin is also available.

Crust

2 cups almonds, soaked

10 Medjool dates, soaked for 1–2 minutes in filtered water

¼ tsp pure vanilla extract

⅛ tsp sea salt

Filling

2½ cups cashews, soaked

4 large ripe bananas

1½ cups Almond Milk

¾ cup agave nectar

⅛ tsp sea salt

6 Tbsp cacao powder

¾ cup coconut butter

3 Tbsp lecithin granules

1 cup Chocolate Sauce

Yield: One 10-inch cake (serves 12–16)
Freshness: 4 days in the fridge or 2 weeks in the freezer

1. For the crust, place the almonds in a food processor and process until finely ground into crumbs. Add the dates, vanilla and sea salt and combine.
2. Press into the bottom of a 10-inch springform pan.
3. For the filling, place all of the filling ingredients, except the coconut butter, lecithin and chocolate sauce in a blender and blend at high speed until the mixture is smooth. Add the coconut butter and lecithin and blend again for 1 to 2 minutes until combined. The final mixture should be completely smooth.
4. Pour over the almond crust. Cover the cake and let it sit in the freezer overnight.
5. Remove the cake from the pan and garnish with chocolate sauce (below), a sprinkle of cacao powder and/or a slice of banana before serving.

Depending on the size of your blender, you may need to blend the filling in two or three batches.

Chocolate Sauce

This is like your favorite chocolate sauce but without the unhealthy ingredients. It also may be a bit richer due to the real chocolate it contains, which gives it more of a dark chocolate taste than a milk chocolate one.

½ cup agave nectar

¼ cup cacao powder

Pinch sea salt

Yield: ½ cup
Freshness: 2 weeks in the fridge

Put this sauce in a squeeze bottle to make decorating with chocolate sauce a breeze.

1. Whisk everything together in a bowl, ensuring no clumps of cacao powder remain. Voilà!

Coffee Cheesecake

A coffee-lover's dream, this richly delicious cheesecake comes drizzled with Chocolate Sauce (page 135) and no jitters, as we use decaffeinated espresso to make this recipe.

Before You Begin: Prepare the Almond Milk (page 5) and Chocolate Sauce (page 135). Soak the almonds and cashews (page xvi).

Crust

2 cups almonds, soaked

10 Medjool dates, soaked for 1–2 minutes
   in hot water

¼ tsp pure vanilla extract

⅛ tsp sea salt

Filling

2½ cups cashews, soaked

1½ cups Almond Milk

¾ cup agave nectar

¾ cup decaffinated espresso

⅛ tsp sea salt

¾ cup coconut butter

3 Tbsp lecithin granules

1 cup Chocolate Sauce

Yield: One 10-inch cake (serves 12–16)
Freshness: 4 days in the fridge or 2 weeks
in the freezer

1. For the crust, place the almonds in a food processor and process until finely ground, like crumbs. Add the dates, vanilla and sea salt and combine.
2. Press into the bottom of a 10-inch springform pan.
3. For the filling, place all of the filling ingredients, except the coconut butter, lecithin and chocolate sauce in a blender and blend at high speed until the mixture is smooth. Add the coconut butter and lecithin and blend again for 1 to 2 minutes until combined. The final mixture should be completely smooth.
4. Pour over the almond crust. Cover the cake and let it set in the freezer overnight.
5. Remove the cake from the pan and garnish with chocolate sauce, a sprinkle of cacao powder or a fresh coffee bean before serving.

Depending on the size of your blender, you may need to blend the filling in two or three batches.

Lemon Cheesecake

This cheesecake has a bright delicate taste on its own but it can be accentuated with a variety of sauces to give it even more fun and flavor. Convincing our customers it has no dairy is our only challenge!

Before You Begin: Prepare the Almond Milk (page 5) and Fruit Sauce (page 139). Soak the almonds and cashews (page xvi).

Crust

2 cups almonds, soaked

10 Medjool dates, soaked for 1–2 minutes
    in hot water

¼ tsp pure vanilla extract

⅛ tsp sea salt

Filling

2½ cups cashews, soaked

1½ cups Almond Milk

1¼ cups fresh lemon juice (about 8 medium
    lemons)

¾ cup agave nectar

2 Tbsp lemon zest

⅛ tsp sea salt

¾ cup coconut butter

3 Tbsp lecithin granules

1½ cups Fruit Sauce

Yield: One 10-inch cake (serves 12–16)
Freshness: 4 days in the fridge or 2 weeks
in the freezer

1. For the crust, place the almonds in a food processor and process until finely ground, like crumbs. Add the dates, vanilla and sea salt and combine.
2. Press down into the bottom of a 10-inch springform pan.
3. For the filling, place all of the filling ingredients, except the coconut butter, lecithin and fruit sauce in a blender and blend at high speed until the mixture is smooth. Add the coconut butter and lecithin and blend again for 1 to 2 minutes until combined. The final mixture should be completely smooth.
4. Pour over the almond crust. Cover the cake and let it set in the freezer overnight.
5. Remove the cake from the pan and garnish with fruit sauce or a slice of lemon.

Depending on the size of your blender, you may need to blend the filling in two or three batches.

Fruit Sauce

The sweetness of this sauce combined with the tart of Lemon Cheesecake (page 137) is a perfect combination. And the colors are beautiful!

¾ cup fruit (raspberries, blueberries or strawberries work best)

2 Tbsp agave nectar

1½ tsp fresh lemon juice

Pinch sea salt

¼–½ tsp psyllium (optional)

Yield: ½ cup
Freshness: 1 week in the fridge

1. Place the fruit, agave nectar and lemon juice in a blender with a pinch of sea salt. Blend until smooth.
2. Add psyllium, ¼ tsp at a time, only if the sauce is too runny. It should be thick enough that you can drizzle it onto something without pooling on the plate.

If you are using frozen fruit, thaw it before blending.

If you find your sauce getting too thick as time goes on, re-blending it with a little bit of lemon juice, agave nectar and/or water fixes it!

Key Lime Tarts

This sweet delight is so beautiful it's a shame to eat it ... but we know you'll find a way. This recipe was the result of dreaming of summer days. We wanted something bright and cheery in color and sweet and tangy in flavor, and the final product is exactly that!

Crust

½ cup almonds, not soaked

1 cup unsweetened shredded coconut

⅓ cup coconut oil

Pinch sea salt

Filling

2 avocados

¾ cup fresh key lime juice (6–8 medium limes)

½ cup agave nectar

½ tsp pure vanilla extract

⅛ tsp sea salt

½ cup coconut oil

1 tsp psyllium

Unsweetened shredded coconut or fresh berries for garnish

Yield: Eight 2½-inch tarts or one 10-inch pie (serves 8)
Freshness: 2–3 days in the fridge

1. For the crust, place the almonds in a food processor and process until ground, like crumbs. Add the coconut, coconut oil and a pinch of salt and combine.
2. Divide this mixture between eight 2½-inch tart pans or a 10-inch pie pan.
3. For the filling, place all of the filling ingredients, except the coconut oil, psyllium and shredded coconut in a blender and blend at high speed until completely smooth.
4. Add the coconut oil and psyllium and blend to combine.
5. Pour over the crust and chill in the fridge uncovered for at least 1 hour.
6. To serve, garnish with shredded coconut and a thin sliver of lime peel.

Chocolate Raspberry Tart

We wanted a rich chocolate dessert for our Valentine's Day guests and this is what we came up with. We first made it with only chocolate filling but found that was too much; it needed a tart-sweet complement. The raspberries were added and voilà, perfection (see photo on page 118).

Before You Begin: Soak the almonds (page xvi).

Crust

½ cup almonds, soaked

1 cup unsweetened shredded coconut

⅓ cup coconut oil

Filling

1½ cups fresh raspberries

2 Tbsp coconut butter

2 Tbsp agave nectar

1 tsp fresh lemon juice

1½ cups cacao powder

1 cup + 2 Tbsp Grade B maple syrup

2 Tbsp coconut oil

½ tsp sea salt

8 fresh raspberries

Yield: 4 individual 4-inch tarts
Freshness: 1 week in the fridge

1. For the crust, place the almonds in a food processor and process until finely ground, like crumbs. Add the shredded coconut and coconut oil and process until combined.
2. Press this mixture into tart shells making sure the crust reaches up the sides.
3. For the filling, place the raspberries, coconut butter, agave nectar and lemon juice in a blender and blend until smooth. Divide equally among the tart shells and chill uncovered in the fridge for 1 hour until set.
4. Place the cacao powder, maple syrup, coconut oil and sea salt in a food processor and process until smooth.
5. After the raspberry layer has set, pour the chocolate layer on top and chill uncovered in the fridge for at least 2 more hours.
6. Garnish each tart with two fresh raspberries before serving.

Pecan Pie

Anyone with a sweet tooth will surely enjoy this rich dessert. The combination of maple syrup and dates results in a sweet, gooey center with just enough crunch from the pecans to satisfy. It goes best with some Vanilla Cardamom Ice Cream (page 148).

2½ cups almonds, not soaked

½ cup agave nectar

1¾ cups pecans, not soaked

60 Medjool dates (about 1¾ cups), soaked for 1–2 minutes in hot water

¾ cup filtered water

½ cup Grade B maple syrup

¼ tsp pure vanilla extract

50 whole pecans

Yield: One 8-inch pie (serves 8)
Freshness: 1 week in the fridge

1. Place the almonds in a food processor and process until ground. Sprinkle 2 Tbsp of the ground almonds on the bottom of an 8-inch pie pan to prevent the pie from sticking.
2. Add the agave nectar to the ground almonds in the food processor and process to combine.
3. Press this mixture down into the prepared pie pan.
4. Place the pecans in a food processor and process until ground.
5. Add the dates and process until a ball forms.
6. Add the water, maple syrup and vanilla and process until smooth.
7. Place the filling evenly on top of the crust and top with whole pecans.

Pumpkin Pie

We've always loved pumpkin pie, and we spent a good amount of time getting this recipe just right. We use butternut squash as it is milder tasting than pumpkin and available to us year-round. We wouldn't want to wait for Thanksgiving to enjoy this favorite pie!

Crust

2½ cups almonds, not soaked

8 Medjool dates, soaked for 1–2 minutes in hot water

¼ tsp sea salt

¼ tsp pure vanilla extract

1–2 Tbsp filtered water

Filling

1 medium butternut squash, shredded (about 3 cups)

1½ cups coconut milk

25 Medjool dates (about ⅔ cup), soaked for 1–2 minutes in hot water

½ cup Grade B maple syrup

1 Tbsp pure vanilla extract

2 tsp ground ginger

2 tsp ground cinnamon

1 tsp ground nutmeg

⅛ tsp ground turmeric

⅛ tsp sea salt

½ cup + 2 Tbsp coconut butter

¼ cup lecithin granules

Yield: One 10-inch pie (serves 8–10)
Freshness: 1 week in the fridge

1. For the crust, place the almonds in a food processor and process until ground. Add the dates, salt and vanilla extract and pulse to combine.
2. Add the water 1 Tbsp at a time if needed to make the crust stick together.
3. Press into the bottom and up the sides of a 10-inch pie pan, ensuring the sides of the crust come right to the top. The upper edge of the crust should be a bit thicker than the bottom.
4. For the filling, peel the butternut squash. Cube it and shred it using the shredding blade on your processor. Measure out 3 cups.
5. Add the squash to the blender with all the other ingredients, except the coconut butter and lecithin, and blend until smooth.
6. Add the coconut butter and lecithin and blend again until completely smooth.
7. Pour into the pie crust and let set in the fridge uncovered for at least 2 hours before cutting.

Maple Walnut Ice Cream

At the restaurant people often look at us in bewilderment when we offer ice cream for dessert. They truly believe ice cream must be made with dairy. But we know that the best ice cream in the world is made dairy-free! We'd wager that in a blind taste test people wouldn't know the difference and would prefer our version! In the vegan world there are many variations of ice cream, whether it's made from soy or almond milk or simply from mashed frozen banana. We think our gourmet version is the most decadent yet most nutritious of them all.

Before You Begin: Soak the cashews (page xvi).

1½ cups coconut milk

¾ cup Grade B maple syrup

1 cup cashews, soaked

½ cup coconut meat

¼ cup filtered water

1 Tbsp pure vanilla extract

½ cup whole walnuts, not soaked

Yield: 4 servings
Freshness: 2 weeks in the freezer

1. Place everything, except the walnuts, in a blender and blend until smooth.
2. Transfer to a stainless steel bowl and place it in the freezer uncovered for 20 minutes.
3. Transfer the mix to an ice-cream maker. Let the machine run for 30 minutes.
4. Chop the walnuts into small pieces and, after 30 minutes, add them to the ice-cream maker while it's running to combine with the other ingredients. Let the walnut pieces incorporate for a minute or so.
5. Transfer the mixture back to the stainless steel bowl and place in the freezer for 20 minutes.
6. Using an ice-cream scoop or spoon, form ice cream into scoops and place in an airtight container. Store in the freezer.
7. To serve, garnish each scoop with a whole walnut or banana slice.

Mint Chocolate Chip Ice Cream

Perhaps the king of desserts! Most people are intimidated at the thought of making this at home, when it is really very simple! Having said that, we spent years experimenting before we settled on this recipe. That's not to say we'll stop tinkering . . . and neither should you. This is one recipe that begs for endless experimentation.

Before You Begin: Prepare the Chocolate Sauce (page 135). Soak the cashews (page xvi).

1½ cups coconut milk

½ cup agave nectar

½ cup cashews, soaked

½ cup coconut meat

¼ cup filtered water

1 Tbsp pure vanilla extract

¼ tsp spirulina, for coloring

1 drop pure peppermint extract

½ cup cacao nibs

½ cup Chocolate Sauce

Yield: 4 servings
Freshness: 1 week in the freezer

1. Place everything, except the cacao nibs and chocolate sauce, in a blender and blend until very smooth.
2. Transfer to a stainless steel bowl and place uncovered for 30 minutes in freezer.
3. Transfer the mix to an ice-cream maker. Let the machine run for 30 minutes.
4. After 30 minutes, add the cacao nibs while the ice-cream maker is running. Let the cacao nibs incorporate with the other ingredients for a minute or so.
5. Transfer the mixture back to a stainless steel bowl and place in the freezer for 20 minutes.
6. Using an ice-cream scoop or spoon, form the ice cream into scoops and place them in an airtight container. Store in the freezer.
7. To serve, garnish with chocolate sauce.

The amount of mint you use depends on the strength of the peppermint extract you're using. Always start with one drop and increase according to taste.

Vanilla Cardamom Ice Cream

This ice cream is the perfect "à la mode." Pair it with our Pumpkin Pie (page 145) or Pecan Pie (page 143), or throw it in a smoothie to make a triple-thick shake!

Before You Begin: Soak the cashews (page xvi).

1½ cups coconut milk

½ cup agave nectar

½ cup coconut meat

½ cup cashews, soaked

¼ cup filtered water

1½ tsp pure vanilla extract

1 tsp vanilla powder

½ tsp ground cardamom

Yield: 4 servings
Freshness: 1 week in the freezer

1. Place all of the ingredients in a blender and blend until smooth.
2. Transfer to a stainless steel bowl and place in the freezer for 20 minutes uncovered.
3. Transfer the mix to an ice-cream maker. Let the machine run for 30 minutes.
4. Transfer the mixture back to a stainless steel bowl and place in the freezer for 20 minutes.
5. Using an ice-cream scoop or spoon, form the ice cream into scoops and place them in an airtight container. Store in the freezer.

Staples

Nut Loaf Patties

These are an extremely versatile and flavorful item that can be used in a multitude of ways. We use them in our Taco and Caesar Wraps (pages 86 and 85) and crumble them into our Bolognese (page 103). We've even crumbled them into our Caesar Salad (page 70) at home for an extra protein boost!

Before You Begin: Soak the sunflower and pumpkin seeds, walnuts and almonds (page xvi). Soak the sun-dried tomatoes in filtered water for two hours. Drain and discard all soaking water.

2½ cups sunflower seeds, soaked

2½ cups pumpkin seeds, soaked

⅓ cup walnuts, soaked

⅓ cup almonds, soaked

⅓ cup sun-dried tomatoes

1¼ portobello mushrooms, chopped small

1 large red bell pepper, chopped small

1 large red onion, chopped small

⅓ cup cilantro

¼ cup + 2 Tbsp extra virgin olive oil

⅓ cup filtered water

3 Tbsp Coconut Aminos

3 cloves garlic

1½ tsp ground cumin

1½ tsp chili powder

1½ tsp onion powder

1½ tsp ground oregano

1½ tsp sea salt

¼ tsp cayenne pepper

Yield: 18 patties
Freshness: 2 weeks in the fridge

1. Line a dehydrator tray with a non-stick sheet.
2. Place all of the ingredients in a food processor and process until just combined. Depending on the size of your food processor, you may have to do this step in two batches.
3. Spread 6 cups of the mixture on the prepared tray.
4. Score into 18 patties as shown.
5. Dehydrate for 12 hours.
6. Flip, remove the non-stick sheet and continue dehydrating for another 6 to 8 hours. When flipping, it is easiest to place a new mesh tray directly on top of the patties and simply turn the two trays over and peel the mesh off. The patties should be firm enough to move without breaking but still slightly moist.

Coconut Aminos can be substituted with tamari or a soy sauce alternative.

Refried "Beans"

This is an all-purpose Southwest-tasting spread that we use in several dishes in the restaurant, including our Nachos (page 31), Taco Salad (page 74), and Mexican Pizza (page 115). They have a little bit of spicy bite to them and reminded us of refried beans . . . hence the name!

8 Medjool dates, soaked for 1–2 minutes in hot water

3 Tbsp sun-dried tomatoes

1 cup walnuts, not soaked

1 stalk celery

½ red bell pepper

½ green onion, except for the bottom ½ inch

2 tsp filtered water

½ tsp Coconut Aminos

½ tsp ground turmeric

½ tsp ground coriander

½ tsp ground cumin

¼ tsp regular paprika

Pinch ground black pepper

Pinch cayenne pepper

Yield: 1½ cups
Freshness: 5 days in the fridge

1. Place the dates and sun-dried tomatoes in a bowl and fill with enough hot water to just cover them. Let them soak for 1–2 minutes to soften and make them easier to process. Drain the water and remove the pits from the dates.
2. Process the walnuts in a food processor until ground. Transfer to a bowl.
3. Process the celery, bell pepper, onion, water, Coconut Aminos, turmeric, coriander, cumin, paprika, black pepper and cayenne pepper, along with the tomatoes and dates, in a food processor until combined. Add the ground walnuts and mix well to combine.

Rawitch Spice Mix

Our long-time manager, Alana Cowl, and I came up with this spice concoction to add a little bite to our Rawitch (page 81). We liked it so much, though, that we started to use it on a variety of items from our Soft Corn Tacos (page 97) to our Avocado Scoop (page 44). And it's a breeze to make . . . .

2 Tbsp sea salt

1½ tsp ground black pepper

1½ tsp cayenne pepper

1 tsp ground cumin

1 tsp chili powder

1 tsp onion powder

Yield: ¼ cup

Freshness: indefinitely in an airtight container

1. Place all of the ingredients in a container and shake to combine.

Almond Cheese

This recipe is very rich in flavor and has a decent kick of spice, but more important, it proves you don't need dairy to make a great cheese spread! We use this mainly in our Taco Wrap (page 86) but it can also be used as a spread for Flatbreads (page 163).

Before You Begin: Soak the almonds (page xvi).

1 cup almonds, soaked

1 clove garlic, minced

1-inch piece ginger, peeled

1 Tbsp white miso

2 tsp extra virgin olive oil

⅛ tsp chili powder

⅛ tsp cayenne pepper

Pinch sea salt

½ cup filtered water

This recipe expands slightly over a few days so leave a little room for this in the container when you're storing it.

Yield: 1½ cups
Freshness: 1 week in the fridge

1. Place everything, except the water, in a food processor and process until it has a pâté-like texture.
2. Add the water and process until smooth.

Cashew Cheese

This basic raw-food staple is simple and versatile—it's used in everything from Sprouted Buckwheat Pizza (page 114) to Beet Ravioli (page 108). Over the years we've added some garlic and freshly ground black pepper to add even more flavor to it.

Before You Begin: Soak the cashews (page xvi).

⅔ cup cashews, soaked

1½ tsp fresh lemon juice

½ clove garlic, chopped

1½ tsp nutritional yeast

½ tsp sea salt

Pinch ground black pepper

¼ cup filtered water

Yield: 1½ cups
Freshness: 4 days in the fridge

1. Place everything, except the water, in a food processor and process until combined.
2. Add the water and process until smooth.

The amount of water you need will depend on how long the cashews have been soaking. Start with ¼ cup and add more to desired consistency.

Pine Nut Parmesan

Unfortunately pine nuts are incredibly expensive but their delicious buttery taste is essential to making this recipe work. We use this to top our Bolognese (page 103) and Caesar Salad (page 70) as it adds a very Parmesan-like flavor! Sprinkle this on anything to add a salty, cheesy flavor.

4 cups pine nuts

¼ cup nutritional yeast

4 tsp sea salt

Yield: 4 cups

Freshness: 2 weeks in the fridge

1. Simply place all of the ingredients in the food processor and pulse to combine. It doesn't take much to over-process this, so be sure to pulse carefully.

Sour Cream

We often have customers request their orders "without the sour cream" because, although they know we are a vegan restaurant, they can't imagine how raw, vegan sour cream could be made! Our Nacho Platter (page 31), Taco Salad (page 74) and Soft Corn Tacos (page 97) would not be complete without it.

Before You Begin: Soak the cashews (page xvi).

¾ cup filtered water

⅓ cup cashews, soaked

½ cup frozen young coconut

1½ Tbsp lemon juice

½ Tbsp apple cider vinegar

½ Tbsp white miso

¼ tsp sea salt

Yield: 1½ cups

Freshness: 1 week in airtight container in fridge

1. Blend on high speed in a blender until completely smooth.

Pizza Crust

The Alissa Cohen–inspired crust is the base we use for a variety of amazing pizzas served at the restaurants. This is one of our favorite meals and has been a mainstay in the restaurant for the last five years. While it takes a little bit of extra preparation time, it is well worth it and friends and family will be really impressed! And the recipe makes three crusts.

Before You Begin: Prepare the buckwheat: Two to three days before you plan to make this, soak 2 cups of buckwheat in warm filtered water for 30 minutes. Drain through the mesh basket and leave in the basket to sprout, rinsing in filtered water every morning and night until sprouts appear. This will give 3 cups sprouted buckwheat. Prepare the flax: Two hours before you plan to make this, soak the flax in 3 cups of filtered water. Do not drain.

3 large carrots

3 cups sprouted buckwheat

1½ cups whole golden flax

½ cup extra virgin olive oil

2 cloves garlic, minced

1 tsp sea salt

1 tsp dried rosemary

1 tsp dried oregano

Yield: 3 crusts
Freshness: 1 week in the fridge

1. Line three dehydrator trays with non-stick sheets.
2. Peel and shred the carrots.
3. Place the shredded carrots with all of the other ingredients in a food processor and process until combined.
4. Spread 3 cups of dough on each prepared dehydrator tray. Using a spatula or your hands, spread the dough into a pizza-crust shape.
5. Dehydrate for 12 hours.
6. Flip, remove the non-stick sheet and continue dehydrating for another 4 to 6 hours, until the crusts are firm but still soft to the touch.

Dipping the spatula or your hands in water while spreading the dough prevents it from sticking!

Burger Buns

It's very difficult to find something fluffy and dough-like to create a bun in the raw-food world but we found that our pizza crust recipe brings us pretty close. Whether you're running a restaurant or cooking at home, it's always helpful if you can find multiple ways to use a recipe.

Before You Begin: Prepare the buckwheat: Two days before you plan to make this, soak ⅔ cup of buckwheat in warm filtered water for 30 minutes. Drain through the mesh basket and leave in the basket to sprout, rinsing every morning and night until sprouts appear. This will give you 1 cup of sprouted buckwheat. Prepare the flax: Two hours before you plan to make this, soak the flax in 1 cup of filtered water. Do not drain.

1 large carrot

1 cup sprouted buckwheat

½ cup whole golden flax

2 Tbsp extra virgin olive oil

1 clove garlic, minced

¼ tsp sea salt

¼ tsp dried rosemary

¼ tsp dried oregano

Yield: 6 buns

Freshness: 2 weeks in an airtight container

1. Line a dehydrator tray with a non-stick sheet.
2. Peel and shred the carrots.
3. Place the shredded carrots with all of the other ingredients in a food processor and process until combined.
4. Spread ⅓ cup of dough per bun on the prepared dehydrator tray. Using a spatula or your hands, spread each piece into a burger-bun shape.
5. Dehydrate for 12 hours.
6. Flip the buns, remove the non-stick sheet and continue dehydrating for another 4 to 6 hours, until the buns are firm but still soft to the touch. When flipping, it is easiest to place a new mesh tray directly on top of the buns, then turn the two trays over and remove the top tray and mesh. You should be able to move them without them breaking.

Dipping the spatula or your hands in water while spreading the dough prevents it from sticking!

Tortillas

The best thing about these, other than their taste, is that they take a fraction of the time that most dehydrated items do. You can eat these on the same day you make them—which is a big deal if you haven't noticed.

¾ cup whole golden flax

1½ cups frozen corn, thawed

¼ cup filtered water

¼ red bell pepper

1 Tbsp fresh lemon juice

1½ tsp chili powder

½ tsp sea salt

Yield: 8 tortillas
Freshness: 1 week in an airtight container

Dipping the spatula or your hands in water while spreading the dough prevents it from sticking! They need to be carefully watched in the dehydrator once they've been flipped as they quickly become too dry. If they do dry out too much, lightly wet them using a spray bottle and allow them to air dry.

1. Line a dehydrator tray with a non-stick sheet.
2. Grind the flax in a blender then transfer it to a mixing bowl.
3. Place all of the other ingredients in a food processor and process until just combined.
4. Add the ground flax and process until just combined.
5. Using a spatula or your hands, spread ¼ cup of dough per tortilla on the prepared tray.
6. Dehydrate for 2 hours.
7. Flip, remove the non-stick sheet and continue dehydrating for another hour or so. When flipping, it is easiest to place a new mesh tray directly on top of the tortillas and simply turn the two trays over and peel the mesh off. When ready, the tortillas should be pliable but not moist.

Herb and Onion Flatbread

This classic raw-food flatbread can be enjoyed in multiple ways: as a cracker or bread for a sandwich, or even cut up as croutons for a salad. At the restaurants, we serve them with dill-infused Cashew Cheese (page 157), Caramelized Onions (page 32) and cherry tomatoes.

⅓ cup sun-dried tomatoes

⅓ cup + ½ cup whole golden flax, not soaked

⅓ cup walnuts, not soaked

1¼ cup sunflower seeds, not soaked

3 medium zucchini, skin on

2 cloves garlic

½ red onion

⅓ cup fresh basil

¾ tsp dried oregano

¾ tsp ground black pepper

¾ tsp sea salt

Yield: 12 pieces
Freshness: 2 weeks in an airtight container

1. Line a dehydrator tray with a non-stick sheet.
2. Place the sun-dried tomatoes in hot water to soak for 10 minutes. Discard the soak water.
3. Grind ⅓ cup of the flax in a blender.
4. Place the walnuts and sunflower seeds in a food processor and process just until ground.
5. Shred 2 zucchini using the shredding blade on your food processor.
6. Place the shredded zucchini in a bowl with the walnuts and sunflower seeds.
7. Using the S blade of the processor, process the third zucchini and the rest of the ingredients except the remaining flax.
8. Add the ½ cup whole flax to the bowl and mix everything together.
9. Spread the entire mixture on the tray edge to edge. Score the mixture into 12 pieces: score one line directly down the middle, then rotate the tray and make two more score lines dividing it into 3 columns. You now have 6 rectangles. Draw a diagonal line down the middle of each rectangle to split it into 2 pieces.
10. Dehydrate for 12 hours. Flip, removing the non-stick sheet. When flipping, it is easiest to place a new mesh tray directly on top of the flatbread and simply turn the two trays over and peel the non-stick sheet off. Continue to dehydrate for another 4 to 6 hours until crispy.

Onion Bread

Onion bread is a raw-food classic. For our version we use Coconut Aminos to add a smoky flavor and ensure it is wheat-free. When we make it in the restaurant, we use 50 pounds of onions, which would reduce everyone to tears until we invested in "onion goggles." They really work! Any tears you shed when you make this will be tears of joy because it's so delicious.

2 cups whole golden flax

2 cups sunflower seeds, not soaked

16 medium white onions

1 cup + 2 Tbsp Coconut Aminos

1 cup extra virgin olive oil

Yield: 16 slices

Freshness: 2 weeks in the fridge

1. Line two dehydrator trays with non-stick sheets.
2. Grind the flax in a blender.
3. Grind the sunflower seeds in a food processor.
4. Combine the ground flax and sunflower seeds in a mixing bowl.
5. Peel the onions then shred them using the shredding blade of your food processor. You can also use a mandoline, or simply slice them very thinly with a knife.
6. Add the onions to the flax-sunflower mixture and toss to mix well.
7. Add the Coconut Aminos and olive oil and mix well to combine.
8. Spread 5 cups of the mixture on each tray evenly. Dehydrate for 12 hours.
9. Flip, remove the non-stick sheet and continue dehydrating for 8 to 12 hours until firm but still moist. When flipping, it is easiest to place a new mesh tray directly on top of the onion bread and simply turn the two trays over and peel the mesh off.
10. Cut each tray into 8 slices of onion bread.

Resources

Information about raw food is everywhere on the Internet. There are blogs dedicated to the raw lifestyle and websites that explain raw food from A to Z. The number of YouTube videos demonstrating raw-food recipes is truly amazing! Anyone can become an expert if they have a few hours to spare and the curiosity to devour and absorb the knowledge. Check out your local bookstore and library, too, for one of the many raw and vegan cookbooks that are available now.

Our advice is to soak up the information and decide what works for you then go and experiment. We've seen plenty of people jump with both feet into a particular diet or way of eating, only to realize it was too extreme for their bodies. Extreme programs can be dangerous, but if you use common sense and always ask yourself if you're feeling good about what you're eating, you'll stay on the right track.

Here are some of the websites we've found useful over the years:

www.upayanaturals.com
Upăya Naturals is an online raw-food superstore that ships to Canada and the United States. It's our go-to company for raw-food staples. This website has everything you could imagine and then some—equipment, books, basic ingredients and prepared food!

www.goneraw.com
This is a great community website that has a ton of recipes, as well as forums on all things raw.

www.welikeitraw.com
Although this blog is no longer being updated you can still visit it for its plethora of information about the raw-food lifestyle, including recipes and posts on how other people incorporate raw food into their lives.

www.happycow.net
Happy Cow is a worldwide directory of vegan and vegetarian restaurants. It's an incredible resource that is helping vegetarians and vegans find healthy food, no matter where they are.

www.meetup.com
One of the easiest ways to learn more about the raw lifestyle is to attend a raw-food potluck. Search the Meetup website for one in your neighborhood—set up your own if there isn't one!—try one of the recipes from this book and get to know some other raw-foodies!

Raising a Raw Dog

While it can be a real challenge to tempt children to try your newly adopted eating style, your pets are very easy converts! When we first brought home our dog, Henry, we knew we couldn't feed him dry kibble. Animals have never been observed cooking their own meals so why would kibble be their food of choice? We were determined to make Henry a raw-food dog.

At first we tried making our own raw pet food, and that lasted one day. A raw, vegan household is no place to be grinding up chicken parts! Then we found a company called Nature's Variety that makes frozen raw meals for pets by combining meat with blueberries, alfalfa sprouts, cod liver oil and other healthy ingredients. Our pooch absolutely loves them so it's a breeze feeding him. Our veterinarian is also very happy that we feed him this way as he is one of the healthiest dogs she sees (and she also feeds her three animals the raw-food way).

Aside from these meat meals, Henry chows down on everything we eat—bananas, apples, blueberries, carrots, green peas, romaine lettuce and red bell peppers are just a few of the things he enjoys. He even has salad for dinner—but without the dressing. We just chop them up roughly for him to chow down on. (Caution: Dogs are allergic to a variety of items such as grapes, onions and chocolate, to name a few. Please reference a complete list before feeding anything to your pet.)

It might take your dog a while to come round to these fruit and vegetable snacks if he isn't used to them, but if you persevere, he'll soon gobble them down in record time! And the benefits of feeding pets this way—a silky coat, clear eyes, fresh smell, perfect weight—mean fewer trips to the veterinarian.

Conversions and Equivalents

Measurement Conversion Chart

IMPERIAL	METRIC
1 tsp	5 mL
1 Tbsp	15 mL
1 cup	250 mL
½ cup	125 mL
¼ cup	60 mL
⅛ cup	30 mL

Handy Equivalents

3 tsp	1 Tbsp
2 Tbsp	⅛ cup
4 Tbsp	¼ cup
8 Tbsp	½ cup
16 Tbsp	1 cup
8 fluid ounces	1 cup

Acknowledgments

So many people have contributed to our success, there are literally too many names to list, but particular thanks go to: Tracy, D'Arcy, Connor and Tracy's family, for their motivation, encouragement and support in the beginning. Robin, who helped so much at the start, and Alana, for picking up the ball. All the staff in the early years—it was so much fun working with you! Our loyal and faithful customers, we thank you for your incredible support over the years. Jack and Lea for their patience, love and faith in making this all come true! Thank you also to Rohit, who shot all the photography in this book using only natural light. Finally, thank you to Robert, Lindsay and Mike, and all the people at Appetite who have helped make this book a reality.

A Word about Franchising

Running a restaurant is by far the most challenging job we've ever had! In the beginning it was the most practical way to eat raw every day, but now it feels like we're answering a lifelong calling. Nothing is more satisfying than waking up every morning knowing we're making this amazing, healthy lifestyle available to as many people as possible.

If you'd like to feel this way, too, then you'll be pleased to know we offer franchises! We're still a small company—just the two of us, in fact, trying to make this happen—and we want to change how people perceive franchising, from both the entrepreneur's and the customers' points of view. If you'd like to find out more, please visit our website (www.rawlicious.ca) or send us an email (info@rawlicious.ca). We'd love to chat with you.

Index